THE NOVELS AND JOURNALS OF FANNY BURNEY

Also by D. D. Devlin

WALTER SCOTT
THE AUTHOR OF WAVERLEY
JANE AUSTEN AND EDUCATION
WORDSWORTH AND THE POETRY OF EPITAPHS
DE QUINCEY, WORDSWORTH AND THE ART OF PROSE

The Novels and Journals of Fanny Burney

D. D. Devlin

Reader in English Literature
The Queen's University of Belfast

St. Martin's Press   New York

© D. D. Devlin, 1987

All rights reserved. For information, write:
Scholarly & Reference Division,
St. Martin's Press, Inc.,
175 Fifth Avenue, New York, NY 10010

First published in the United States of America in 1987

Printed in Hong Kong

ISBN 0–312–00034–0

Library of Congress Cataloging-in-Publication Data
Devlin, D. D. (David Douglas)
The novels and journals of Fanny Burney.
Bibliography: p.
Includes index.
1. Burney, Fanny, 1752–1840. 2. Novelists,
English—18th century—Biography. 3. Great Britain—
Court and courtiers—Biography. I. Title.
PR3316.A4Z59 1987   823'.6 [B]   86–15569
ISBN 0–312–00034–0

To
Jonathan
who kept me right about France
and the French Revolution

Contents

List of Abbreviations

ED   *The Early Diary of Frances Burney 1768–1778, with a Selection from her Correspondence and from the Journals of her Sisters Susan and Charlotte Burney*, ed. Annie Raine Ellis (2 vols, 1889), reprinted by Bell (2 vols, 1913).

Diary   *Diary and Letters of Madame d'Arblay*, ed. Charlotte Barrett (7 vols, 1842–6). References are to the new edition of 1854.

Journals   *The Journals and Letters of Fanny Burney*, ed. Joyce Hemlow and others, 12 vols (Oxford, 1972–84).

1
Introductory

The dates of her novels are important: *Evelina* was published in 1778 when Fanny Burney was twenty-six years old; *Cecilia* came out in 1782, *Camilla* in 1796; and *The Wanderer*, which was largely written in France between 1802 and 1812, was published in 1814, two years after her return to England. The first two novels were written before the French Revolution, the third in the aftermath of the Terror and the fourth during her ten-year exile in Napoleon's France. In her long life as a novelist and her much longer life as a person (she was born in 1752 and died in 1840) Fanny Burney moved from the age of Dr Johnson, who taught her Latin, to the restoration of Louis XVIII who rewarded her husband, M. d'Arblay, for his loyal service in the campaign of 1814–15 by conferring upon him the title of *comte*, by making him a Lieutenant-General and by awarding him a pension.

The first two novels were published before her five weary, desolate years at Court from 17 July 1786 to 7 July 1791 as Second Keeper of the Queen's Robes, and before she met her future husband in 1793. These five years at Court were (oddly) the period of her greatest isolation from public events. John Galt in *Annals of the Parish* makes fun of the Rev. Micah Balwhidder's journal entry for the year 1789:

> This I have always reflected upon as one of our blessed years. It was not remarkable for any extraordinary occurrence, but there was a hopefulness in the minds of men, and a planning of new undertakings . . .

Mr Balwhidder was living in a remote parish in Ayrshire; but 400 miles to the south another journal writer was equally unaware of the dramatic happenings in France. Fanny Burney was with the King and Queen in Weymouth on the 14 July 1789, but her detailed journal-letters to her father (Dr Burney) in that summer contain no reference to events in France. It is not until the end of October that she mentions the Bastille and

1

the sudden adversity of the French. Truly terrible and tremendous are revolutions such as these. There is nothing in old history that I shall any longer think fabulous; the destruction of the most ancient empires on record has nothing more wonderful, nor of more sounding improbability, than the demolition of this great nation, which rises up all against itself for its own ruin – perhaps annihilation

(ED, v, 53–4)

Such unawareness was untypical. Before her court appointment she lived in London with her father, and through him she met and was friendly with many literary and political figures of the day – Johnson, Burke, Mrs Thrale, Horace Walpole, William Wyndham, Joshua Reynolds and David Garrick – but her diaries and letters contain little political comment and even less political interest.

In 1788 Fanny Burney was given tickets by the Queen to attend the trial of Warren Hastings and on several later occasions she was allowed to repeat her visits. Her accounts of the trial are lengthy and vivid and delighted the King and Queen who sent her back to hear Hastings' defence in 1790. It was not the politics which interested her; she regarded the prosecution as a party affair and saw the trial as a kind of grand theatre in which some of her close friends were involved. She supported Hastings partly because she knew him, partly because her sister Charlotte's husband, Clement Francis, had at one time been secretary to Warren Hastings in India, and partly because she was sure of his innocence – she felt "a strong internal evidence" of it drawn "from all I have seen of him". She felt a thrill of dismay when she saw "Mr Burke as Head of the Managers of the Prosecution make his solemn entry" and she grieved to see her old friend as "now the cruel Prosecutor . . . of an injured and innocent man!". But she saw it only as drama; she was interested only because her friends were involved. She sat inside Westminster Hall but saw the trial from the outside with her sharp, observant eyes. It was the 1790s that changed Fanny Burney as they changed so many others. In March 1790 the Queen read to her "a part of a speech of Mr Burke upon the revolution in France, and then she lent it me to finish". This was Burke's speech on the Army Estimates and his first public attack on the principles of the Revolution. In November 1790 (the month of its publication) Fanny Burney read his *Reflections on the French Revolution* and found it "the noblest, deepest, most animated, and exalted work" that she had ever read. The year 1790 was a quiet one in France; "the worst excesses of the French Revolution", the September massacres, the attack on the Tuileries and the killing of the Swiss Guard, the execution of the King and Queen, the Reign of Terror and the guillotinings, were still to come. But Fanny Burney with her "imagination of disaster" and her intense personal loyalty to the King and Queen of England is already fearing what she calls "the many-headed mob".

In July 1791 she was released from the bondage of her court position, and in August, to recover her health, went off on a three-week jaunt to the West of England. At Winchester she met for the first time a party of four French refugees. They were having trouble with accommodation; but although Fanny Burney and her friend "were now touched to shake off a part of the John Bullism that had encrusted us, and to ask them to our sitting room, to drink tea", her sympathy was still not great. She saw them as exotic and strange and was delighted that one of the ladies "seemed exactly a French character drawn by an English author". They were, it seems, aristocrats and *plus royalistes que le roi* since they blamed the "unguarded laxity" of the King for the anarchy of France. Fanny Burney, however, sees the position in France as "a change of despotism" and "a demolition of tyranny by tyranny". She rejoices, she says, to see those redressed who have been injured, but feels horror "to see those oppressed who are guiltless". What remained of her "John Bullism" was soon to be shattered; her political awareness and her long involvement with France were about to begin.

In October 1792 she tells of a whole day's talk on French politics with Arthur Young, the author of *Travels in France* (1792) and a connection of the Burney family. Young had very much abandoned his earlier radical opinions and was now particularly harsh on what he called the "constituant *révolutionnaires*". This is a reference to the Moderates or Constitutionalists who were in varying degrees loyal to the King but who, like Mirabeau, wished to give France a constitution on the British model. Mirabeau had died in April 1791, two months before the King's attempted escape from Paris and his flight to Varennes; but another constitutionalist, Lafayette, the French hero of the American War of Independence, had connived at the escape. He and others of the new moderates formed the "Feuillant" party in the Constituent Assembly, but in July 1791 their influence was weakened when Lafayette's National Guard shot and killed fifty demonstrators in the Champ de Mars. The largest group in the new Legislative Assembly was composed of members of the Feuillant club; but by the Spring of 1792 their influence was over, their ability to protect the King was doubtful and power was passing to the Girondins and Jacobins. In the summer Lafayette and the Feuillants were making preparations for the King's flight to Rouen or Compiègne, but the attack on the Tuileries in August and the September massacres which followed destroyed their credibility. The Feuillant ministry collapsed, its members fled and a provisional executive council of Girondins and Jacobins was established with Danton as its effective head. At the outbreak of war in April of the same year Lafayette had been given command of a French army at Metz; on the 17 August he deserted to the Austrians. Other Constitutionalists or Feuillants escaped to England. Among them was the Comte Louis de Narbonne (an illegitimate son of Louis XV) who through his friendship with Lafayette had been given command of the professional *corps d'élite* of the National Guard at Paris and who brought with him from France his mistress Madame de Staël. Others who arrived in the summer of 1792 were the Comte de Liancourt (an old acquaintance of Arthur Young), the devious Talleyrand and the very undevious M. d'Arblay. D'Arblay was a Constitutionalist who had been Adjutant-General to Lafayette but was not an *émigré* of political importance. He had been the officer in charge of the guard at the Tuileries on the night of the King's escape to Varennes and, it seems, had been in great danger of being denounced and even massacred, though he always claimed that he had been kept in ignorance of the King's intention.

These were some of the Constitutionalists who after escapes and hurried journeys were glad to reach England and (except for Liancourt) to settle at Juniper Hall near the village of Mickleham in Surrey. England gave them a haven but scarcely a welcome, though Fanny Burney's friends, the Lockes, who lived close by, received them hospitably. The Constitutionalists had failed, but in England they were blamed for more than failure. In June 1792 Liancourt "began to see that the Monarch or the Jacobins must inevitably fall, and he could scarce support the prospect of ultimate danger threatening the former".[1] But it was too late for repentance or realism; the Moderates were blamed for the past, increasing and future violence of events in France through having ever attempted to limit the powers of the King. Arthur Young thought that Liancourt deserved all his personal misfortunes since "he has brought it all on himself, and what is worse, on his Country".[2]

There is no need to trace the myriad shifts and shades of political position and opinion of all those who might be called Moderates. The terms used to describe them before and since, Constitutionalists, Feuillants, Monarchists, Democrats, were blanket terms; but with the lessening of English sympathy for them and with the growing anxiety in England about the way things were going in France, these people were inevitably blanketed. They had let a dreadful genie out of the bottle; it was they and not the genie who were blamed, and it was not a time for nice distinctions and definitions. *The Times* revealed this growing impatience and showed how all subleties and distinctions were lost in anger when in August 1792, shortly before the arrival of the French *émigrés* at Juniper Hall, it divided French political parties into three: Royalists, Republicans and Monarchists: "Those of the FIRST party are for *restoring the King*. Those of the SECOND are *for no King*. Those of the THIRD want to have a nominal King, *without any power*." For *The Times* a more accurate term for Royalists would be *"faithful subjects"*, and for such Republicans as Robespierre and Danton, "obscure rascals". (*The Times* admitted that the Duc d'Orléans, though a rascal, was not obscure.) The chief target for *The Times* was, however, "The Monarchists, who ought rather to be styled ANTI-MONARCHISTS" and who

> also call themselves Feuillans. . . . At the head of this party are almost all the Ministers of that unfortunate King who is surrounded by traitors, and with them are La Fayette . . . the Bishop d'Autun [Talleyrand] Rochefoucault [cousin of de Liancourt]. . . . This party, which is beyond all doubt the most dangerous, being the most seducing, is every day gaining ground.

(In fact, though *The Times* did not know it, the power of the Monarchists had failed.) It then sarcastically allowed a fourth category:

> Some known by the appelation CONSTITUTIONALISTS, profess an inviolable attachment to the Constitution decreed by the National Assembly; and allow, at the same time, that, in many particulars, it is susceptible to many modifications . . .

(Journals, ii, xi–xii)

This flexibility made them dangerous.

These were the kind of people whom Fanny Burney was shortly to meet when she visited her friends the Lockes in Norbury Park close to Juniper Hall in January 1793. Arthur Young had arranged a meeting for her with de Liancourt who had read *Cecilia* and had long hoped to see her. From her sister at Norbury Park she was eagerly learning details of the new arrivals and was already beginning to love them for the dangers they had passed. And she quickly knew to be discreet in talking to others about them, for she now understood (as she told her sister) that in the general opinion *"All* the *Constituents"* (by which she meant the Constitutionalists or Moderates) "are now reviled as authors and originators of all the misfortunes of France, from arrogant self sufficiency in their powers to *stop,* as well as *begin,* when they pleased".[3] She admits that she herself had shared this dislike and had been "the foe of all their proceedings while in power"; but she now finds them "truly attractive" because of their distresses and because of that continuing loyalty to the King which had taught them the folly of compromise with revolution. When she actually met them some weeks later in January 1793 she found them more attractive still. She was, in spite of herself, dazzled and charmed by Talleyrand ("It is inconceivable what a convert M. de Talleyrand has made of me") but could shrewdly note that "He is a man of admirable conversation, quick, terse, *fin,* and yet deep". (Depth would become deception after his expulsion from England in the Spring of 1794.) The Comte de Narbonne is all refinement, elegance, repartee and wit, and "bears the higher character for goodness". She finds Mme de Staël at her first meeting "delightful" and at the second the most charming person she has ever seen. Once again she notes her "depth", finds her a "profound politician" but is won over completely by Mme de Staël's love for her father, M. Necker, and by her obvious affection for the authoress of the novels *Evelina* and *Cecilia* which alone (Mme de Staël assured her) had "soothed and regaled" M. Necker in his deep dejection at events in France. Then there was M. d'Arblay. She finds no depth here, indeed, but a simple "openness" and "probity" and "a sincerity, a frankness . . . that I had been unjust enough to think could not belong to a French man".[4] She liked and defended them all ("I am always exposing myself to the wrath of John Bull when the coterie come into competition") but was prepared to face John Bull's wrath and the disappointment of her father (whose opinions were close to John Bull's) when she rapidly fell in love with d'Arblay and married him some months later at the end of July.

"They are," said Fanny Burney of them all, "a marvellous set for excess of agreeability", but, as soon became clear, less marvellous for probity and openness. Inside a fortnight Dr Burney was telling her what he had heard from Burke, that Mme de Staël "has been accused of partiality to M. de Narbonne". It was, in fact, rather more than partiality, for by 1793 she had borne him two sons. Fanny Burney's reaction was to call these stories "a gross calumny" and a thing impossible to be true since "She is very plain; – he is very handsome; – her intellectual endowments must be with him her sole attraction." And, in any case, Mme de Staël seems equally attached to Talleyrand, and she loves the Comte de Montmorency as a brother; and, in short, "her whole coterie live together like brethren". Nevertheless, Fanny Burney took her father's hint that she ought not to stay under the same roof with Mme de Staël now that there was even the shadow of such a rumour. When the shadow was given substance and the fact of the liaison was confirmed by d'Arblay, Fanny Burney, with that fear of giving offence to those she loved and so of losing that love, and that embarrassment at trivially awkward social occasions which she was to dramatize in scene after scene in her novels, wondered in letters of vexed comedy how she could avoid being seen in the company of such adulterous democrats; for it was made clear to her that the moral and political corruption went together. Her "imagination of disaster" suggested that worse might follow. Mme de Staël had talked of her friendship with Dr Burney's daughter and had called at his house in Chelsea; Narbonne had offered to spend a day at Chelsea, possibly even at the same time, and all these friendships and intimacies might reach Royal ears.

How will all this then be blazoned! – and how duped is the unsuspecting Character who fancies she has made a friend! I am inexpressibly disturbed by the expectation of this event's spreading to Q[een's] H[ouse] and occasioning fresh terrors – perhaps injunctions! perhaps *displeasure* . . .

(Journals, ii, 34)

Here, indeed, (at the age of forty-one, it is true) is "The History of a Young Lady's Entrance into the World" (the sub-title of *Evelina*), a world of foreigners, political and amorous intrigue, vexation, embarrassment, romance and "Female Difficulties" (the sub-title of *The Wanderer*). "What in the World can I do?", Fanny Burney asks. The first thing was flight; by keeping clear of London and Surrey she must avoid all chance of further meetings. Next her friends and family not only wished the friendship to cease but they compelled her to appear "its wilful renouncer". She tried in vain to soften Mme de Staël's pique and displeasure at the timorous, fastidious behaviour which in England seemed to be required of a young unmarried woman. Mme de Staël could not understand it and complained to Fanny Burney's married sister that Fanny was behaving like a girl of fourteen. Fanny Burney was "very much vexed at the whole business" but was relieved when Mme de Staël departed for Switzerland a few weeks later in May 1793.

No parental displeasure, however, and no fear of giving offence to family and friends (or even to the King and Queen) could dissuade her from marriage that summer to M. d'Arblay, a penniless Roman Catholic and a distrusted Constitutionalist from a country with which England was already at war. An anxious, even prudish, respect for conventional public manners and morality at no time affected her tough independence of spirit. (In fiction she resembles another Fanny, Fanny Price in *Mansfield Park* whose anxious conformity in conduct could not make her sin against her affections.) From this quarrel of conventionality with freedom, this tension of diffidence and daring, Fanny Burney made drama in her novels. It was d'Arblay's poverty which worried Dr Burney most and not his politics, unless these should cause the Queen to be displeased at the marriage of her former Assistant Keeper of the Robes. It was clear to all, however, that d'Arblay was not a political person. Unlike Talleyrand (in whom he could find no guile) and other *émigrés*, he had at no time come under the suspicion of the British government. His simplicity and integrity were obvious and Fanny Burney was quick to tell her father of d'Arblay's regret for his earlier opinions when news reached England of the King's execution in January: "*I* – scarce can endure my life from the simple feeling of *regret* that ever I pronounced the word LIBERTY – IN FRANCE!"[5] The killing of the King and d'Arblay's simple, shocked repentance now released and made more powerful the full flow of Fanny Burney's natural conservatism. She is anxious for her black gown to be sent to her so that she may put on mourning for the "martyred" King whose end was "saint-like"; and with a reference to Burke she now concludes that

New *Systems*, I fear, in States, are always dangerous, if not wicked; Grievance by grievance, wrong by wrong, must only be assailed, and breathing time allowed to old prejudices, and old habits, between all that is done.

(*Journals*, ii, 3)

She writes a pamphlet to raise money for the 6000 dispossessed and refugee French clergy now living in poverty in England, and upsets some readers by calling them "holy martyrs". France had declared war on England in February and d'Arblay later offered to serve in the Toulon campaign. His offer was declined but his loyalty was made plain: "to his *King*", he said, "and a *limitted Monarchy* he would offer, – O but too willingly – his services and his life". And so it came about that the Queen and all the Royal Family wished her happiness on her marriage to the loyalist, royalist exile, M. d'Arblay. Not all the Queen's subjects were equally forgiving, and her marriage to a Frenchman may have had some effect on the sales of *Camilla* which she now began to write. John Thorpe in *Northanger Abbey* is anybody's fool, but his very different reaction was probably common enough. He found *Camilla* "a stupid book"; and he knew why: "I guessed what sort of stuff it must be before I saw it: as soon as I heard she had married an emigrant, I was sure I should never be able to get through it."[6]

The dates of the novels are, then, important. The first two were written in time of peace and the third and fourth in time of war. As she wrote *Camilla* between 1793 and 1796 Fanny Burney and her husband lived quietly in a cottage not far from Mickleham. It was, nevertheless, for her a time of fear. She feared that her husband might be deported as Talleyrand was in the Spring of 1794. She was alarmed at the rumour which reached the King that her husband had fought alongside Lafayette in America against England, and she dissuaded him from even brief visits to London where the movements of all exiles were watched. She feared for her country and was delighted with her brother's suggestions (made early in 1794) for the defence of England against invasion. In these years when political opinion in England about events in France hardened, the *Critical Review* found her own political views "too Aristocratic". When she heard that Danton and Desmoulins who had voted for the King's execution had themselves been guillotined, she rejoiced "For the *Royal* murderers summarily rewarded in kind." With political reaction came moral reaction and sharper, less generous views of female decorum and behaviour. Fanny Burney never lost her liking for Mme de Staël but could never "vindicate nor esteem nor respect her"; and when she read her *De l'influence des passions sur le bonheur des individus et des nations* (1796) she found that in it "All sort of principle yields to impassion and impulse. She seems to have no idea of any moral *decency*." Mme de Staël, however, was in good company; for at about the same time Fanny Burney was suggesting that even the Old Testament might be corrupting for girls "on account of the fault of the Translators, in not guarding it from terms and expressions impossible – at least utterly improper, to explain".

In November 1800 d'Arblay learnt that following the overthrow of the Directory by Napoleon one year earlier, his name had been erased from the list of *émigrés* and that he was now free to return to France without fear of persecution. Some small remaining property might now be saved from sequestration if he would go to France, and by good fortune the peace concluded between England and France in October 1801 gave d'Arblay the chance to travel to France and attempt to salvage what remained of the family fortune. The Queen approved of his departure and of his wife's wish to go with him. By the beginning of November d'Arblay was in France where he was warned that he must stay for a year before returning to England, and in the Spring of 1802 Fanny Burney joined him in Paris. She did not believe that her stay in France or the peace with France would last for long, for her opinion of Napoleon was tough and simple: "I think him so vindictive and such a man of blood, that his reign will be severe and, consequently, short." But her husband's effort to secure either property or a pension or a place delayed their return until return was made impossible by the outbreak of war. Impossible – or, at least, very difficult. As the years passed she became more and more desperate to see her ageing, ailing father, but it was not until 1812 that she was able to board at Dunkirk an American ship which was to call illicitly at Dover. She brought with her to England her son Alex, aged seventeen, and the manuscript of her fourth novel, *The Wanderer*. Her years in France were in many ways happy; she was welcomed by a large circle of d'Arblay's friends; she was fêted everywhere as a novelist, and her husband was known in Napoleon's phrase as "the husband of Cecilia". Her journals and letters for her ten years of exile make no complaints and suggest no painful regrets. It was not until 1815 that she confessed that in those ten years "my mind was a stranger to rest"; and it was years after the death of her husband that she called her forced absence from England "a constant worm that eat, even then, into my peace of mind". *The Wanderer*, her last novel, was the product of those ten, tense, difficult years.

It is unlikely that four novels spanning the thirty-six years from 1778 to 1814 should be merely variations on a theme and show no shift of interest or emphasis. Fanny Burney had read Burke on the French Revolution and had listened to him in countless political discussions; she had met and mixed with distinguished French *émigrés*, and had married one of them; she had spent ten years in Napoleon's France with a husband who had loyalties to two countries; she had become familiar with the English Jacobin novel of the 1790s (she read *Caleb Williams* in 1796) and with the arguments of the English Radicals (at the very least she knew of Paine's *Rights of Man* and Mary Wollstonecraft's *Vindication of the Rights of Woman*). It is impossible that in her fiction she should not have betrayed a deepening political awareness or not have shown any change of position in that other war of the 1790s, the war of ideas.[7] Yet the only change that contemporary reviewers found was change for the worse. The vast success of *Evelina* was partly to blame. Fanny Burney was at once called a female Richardson, Fielding and Smollett; Mrs Thrale found *Evelina* "a boisterous book"; Dr Johnson praised its "knowledge of life and manners" and "accuracy of observation"; reviewers admired above all her comic characters, and she became established as, in Johnson's phrase, "a character monger". When her later novels had the same merits they were praised, but when they hadn't they weren't. It was not even noticed that Fanny Burney had signalled a change by not wishing to call her third and fourth books "novels", and critics made it more difficult to see her development by not troubling to read *The Wanderer*. William Hazlitt in his lecture "On the English Novelists" (1819) mentions but does not discuss it. Certainly its political implications and its keener awareness of the position of women should have made it impossible to find her only a comic writer. As it is, she is for him now an old-fashioned writer, "quite one of the old school, a mere common observer of manners" one of those who "amidst the tumult of events crowded into this period" have "kept the even tenor of their way". For Hazlitt *Evelina* is the best because the shortest; when she repeated herself in *Cecilia* and *Camilla* she did it badly. If these two are different it is only because they are longer and duller through "the tediousness of the story". When he complains that the "Female Difficulties" of her heroine in *The Wanderer* are created out of nothing, it is, perhaps, time to wonder what greater difficulty Hazlitt has in mind than the heroine's escape from the Terror in France to England in a small boat when the two countries were at war.

For Macaulay, too, the movement is downwards. Writing in 1843 he finds that Fanny Burney's strength is in human characters and that the best of these are to be found in *Evelina* and *Cecilia*. The only point of her clumsy plots is to exhibit "striking groups of eccentric characters, each governed by his own peculiar whim, each talking his own peculiar jargon". In *The Wanderer* it is possible to catch only a gleam of her greatness; it does not suffer from "decay of power, but from a total perversion of power".[8] A hundred years later not much has changed. For Lord David Cecil Fanny Burney is still "a bright, light, humorous observer of the outward scene" with a special gift for noting those social distinctions which are "the dominant subject of her stories". *Camilla* and *The Wanderer*, because they are not bright and light and humorous, "show a decline in every respect" and have nothing new to offer but an aggressive moralism and stilted language.[9] Even Joyce Hemlow does not distinguish between the earlier and later novels: all are equally (but not equally good) displays of courtesy-book morals in action. When she claims that the forwarding action in all the novels is "felicitous behaviour" and the retarding action "infelicitous behaviour" she in fact describes only *Evelina* and *Cecilia*; and when she says that in Fanny Burney's fiction "the young hero combines the roles of monitor and lover" she describes none of the novels at all.[10]

The confusion of change with decay is continued by Fanny Burney's most recent editors, Lillian D. and Edward A. Bloom. For them the first two novels are "dazzlingly successful" while the last two have vanished "into literary non-existence". Where others found stylistic reasons for failure the Blooms find psychological and autobiographical ones. *Evelina* and *Cecilia* succeeded because she "needed to be pulled by an inner tension, torn between a fairy tale world she envisioned for herself and the frustration and uncertainties with which she lived". Conflict made for success; she therefore wished to repeat herself, but *The Wanderer* could not succeed since "her ten years in France were for the most part without conflict".[11] "She was," declares Joyce Hemlow, "more than most writers *present* in history and industriously she recorded it for family, friends and posterity";[12] but this seems to mean simply that Fanny Burney was in Paris the day before Napoleon entered it and

in Brussels when Waterloo was fought and that she was chased by
George III in Kew Gardens. And yet she remained (and remains)
"quite of the old school", miraculously untouched by the mighty
"tumult of events" domestic and foreign through which she lived
from 1789 to 1815. Thanks to the superb Hemlow edition of Fanny
Burney's *Journals and Letters* we now know more of the tumult –
intellectual, political and social – that was her everyday experience
and of her changing response to the spirit of the age. She was by
nature a conservative, but her reactions are neither simple nor
predictable, and she is not to be caught in the crisp categories of
jacobin or anti-jacobin novelist. She observed much more than
manners and had an ear for more than colloquial speech. It is absurd
to see her (alone of all writers of the period) as somehow bearing no
mark of "the unimaginable touch of time" or of the times. It is the
very touch of time which she knew about profoundly as a person
and which she sharply imagined as a novelist.

When *The Wanderer* appeared in March 1814 the publisher's
advertisements at the end for novels already published or novels
soon to appear named, with nice timing, *Waverley* as a novel "In the
Press". But *The Wanderer* is already itself a new departure, an
historical novel.

2
Fact and Fiction

Fanny Burney came to fiction via fact. Jane Austen's Juvenilia made ready the way for the novels, and the Gondal stories were the early imaginative writings of the Brontës. Fanny Burney, it is true, had written a novel (later destroyed) by the age of fifteen, but in the following ten years her preparation for *Evelina* (1778) and *Cecilia* (1782) was the endless writing of diaries, letters and journal-letters. The earlier writers in whom Jane Austen was widely read were the satiric spur to her own first fictions and made her a novelist. She cannot be disentangled from her literary ancestors since it was they who set free her greatness and originality. Fanny Burney was not in this sense a literary writer. She had, of course, read English and French novels (Marivaux was a favourite) but she did not imitate them or make them any part of herself, even by rejection. In spite of what contemporary readers said, there is little sign of Richardson or Fielding in her work. Smollett, indeed, appears in *Evelina*, but this was a short-lived influence, a mistake in direction which she did not repeat. She is very much the individual talent not greatly affected by tradition; as Dr Johnson said after reading *Evelina*, "What she is, she is intuitively." She was not, in fact, much interested in fiction or in the theory of fiction (references to plays and visits to the theatre far outnumber references to novels in her journals) and as the years passed she read fewer and fewer novels and scarcely any by her contemporaries. In the musical Burney family there were other interests and her father's substantial library contained only one novel, Fielding's *Amelia*. She was a disappointment to literary ladies at a party in 1782 when she confessed that they "mentioned to me a hundred novels that I had never heard of"; and a list of books she had read in 1806 or proposed to read in the following year contains scarcely any fiction. There is no sign that she had read or heard of Jane Austen, and her references to Scott's novels are few and unexcited.

It was Fanny Burney the diarist who gave birth to the novelist. She was not at all sure that such a birth was proper and she wrote her novels (though increasingly reluctant to call them that) with a mixture of doubt and daring, and remained all her life ambivalent about novels and the practice of fiction. When Jane Austen vigorously defended the novel in *Northanger Abbey* and particularly mentioned *Cecilia* and *Camilla* as works which have "only genuis, wit and taste to recommend them", she attacked not only the "common cant" of novel-readers who affected not to read novels and decried the capacity and undervalued the labour of the novelist, but also (more interestingly)

> . . . that ungenerous and impolite custom so common with novel writers, of degrading by their contemptuous censure the very performances, to the number of which they are themselves adding – joining with their greatest enemies in bestowing the harshest epithets on such works, and scarcely ever permitting them to be read by their own heroine . . . I cannot approve of it. . . . Let us not desert one another; we are an injured body.[1]

The rebuke could be levelled at Fanny Burney. Novels were not quite the thing and yet she wrote them. There is no kind of writer, she says, so low as "the humble Novelist", yet she was determined to become one. She may not have read much fiction but her heroines read less, and, indeed, it was hard to be a novel-reader *and* a heroine. It wasn't just the moral shadiness of reading novels; too much reading of fiction could alter your appearance. Lady Aurora in *The Wanderer* had "soft expressive blue eyes, of which the 'liquid lustre' spoke a heart that was the seat of sensibility; yet not of that weak romantic cast, formed by early and futile love-sick reading, either in novels or poems".[2]

Fanny Burney's early, embarrassed fear at daring to be a novelist is described in the "Dedication" (to her father) of *The Wanderer*:

> So early was I impressed myself with ideas that fastened degradation to this class of composition, that at the age of adolescence, I struggled against the propensity which, even in childhood, even from the moment I could hold a pen, had impelled me into its toils; and on my fifteenth birth-day, I made so resolute a conquest over an inclination at which I blushed, and that I had always kept secret, that I committed to the flames

whatever, up to that moment, I had committed to paper . . .
   The passion, however, though resisted, was not annihilated: my bureau was cleared; but my head was not emptied; and, in defiance of every self-effort, Evelina struggled herself into life.

(*The Wanderer*, I, xx–xxi)

The nervous sense of degradation and daring is clear in the Preface to *Evelina*. Oddly and snobbishly the degradation comes in part from being widely read; no form of literature has readers "more numerous but less respectable". More is worse; how much better morally to have fit audience though few! Novelists (in the Preface) are by definition writers of "inferior rank", yet a few just men can be found among them to save the whole trade from "contempt" and "depravity". Fanny Burney's list of these saviours contains some surprises but no women: Rousseau and Johnson (with apologies for ranking them as novelists), Fielding, Richardson and Smollett are the great and the good whom, with "a very singular mixture of timidity and confidence", she is now attempting to follow. Or rather, *not* to follow. We may smile at her timidity but the confidence and daring are real and impressive. She will not follow, she says, where they have trod; the path is plain, but they have "left it barren", and, in any case "imitation cannot be shunned too sedulously; for the very perfection of a model which is frequently seen, serves but more forcibly to mark the inferiority of the copy". All this is not mere modesty. She will not follow them but will strike out on her own, will do something new. These are not her phrases, for the mixture of timidity and confidence is in her very syntax as she asserts and withdraws, says yea and says nay.

I have, therefore, only to entreat, that my own words may not pronounce my condemnation, and that what I have here ventured to say in regard to imitation, may be understood, as it is meant, in a general sense, and not be imputed to an opinion of my own originality, which I have not the vanity, the folly, or the blindness, to entertain.

(*Evelina*, Preface, p. 9)

She has been too easily taken at her word. This passage is almost in code; the defensive, evasive insistence of remarks like these is often her way of being independent (she seldom conceals or asserts herself through irony). And, after all, the confidence is greater than the timidity: the Preface is followed by the novel.

She does not imitate Fielding, but she can avoid the degradation if she listens to his advice and follows his example. Fanny Burney has little interest in the novel form, but she found Fielding's views on novel-writing congenial and seems to lean on his Preface to *Joseph Andrews*. Fielding there distinguishes his novel "from the productions of romance writers" (and incidentally insists that he is writing something "hitherto unattempted in our language"). Fanny Burney, too, disclaims all intention of writing Romance, where there is no probability and from which "Reason is an outcast." (Many years later she will be insisting that *Camilla* "is not a Romance".) And she is close to Fielding's mocking description of his novel as "a comic epic poem in prose" when she agrees that *Camilla* is in the "prose Epic Style" and, more solemnly in the Dedication to *The Wanderer*, when she calls her novel a modern epic. Her taste had never been for Romance. In 1768, when she was sixteen, and ten years before the publication of *Evelina*, she says of a work of fiction that it is

so romantick, that every word betrays improbability, instead of disguising fiction, and displays the author, instead of human nature. For my own part, I cannot be much pleased without an appearance of truth; at least of possibility – I wish the story to be natural tho' the sentiments are refined; and the characters to be probable tho' their behaviour is excelling.

(*ED*, I, 9)

The value of *Cecilia*, she argues in 1782, is in its probability, with hero and heroine made neither impossibly miserable nor inhumanly happy: "Is not such a middle state more natural, more according to real life, and less resembling every other book of fiction."[3] And after dismissing in the Dedication to her final work all "merely romantic love-tales" or stories of "improbable wonders", she declares that a novel ought to be "a picture of supposed, but natural and probable human nature". Of course, when Fanny Burney writes in the Preface to *Evelina* that her intention is "to draw characters from nature, though not from life, and to mark the manners of the times" and uses the phrase "real life" to define the subject of *Cecilia* and talks of *The Wanderer* as a picture of "natural . . . human nature", she is not suggesting that fiction should offer a naïve mimesis or surface realism. She is using the neo-classical language of Fielding (a language she never renounced) and very nearly the same phrases. In *Joseph Andrews* "everything is copied from the book of nature", and the only provision in *Tom Jones* is "no other than *Human Nature*". Fielding describes "not men, but manners, not an individual, but a species". Fanny Burney's objection to a novel that it "displays the author instead of human nature" is the Johnsonian rejection of "singularity". While she and Fielding do not mean the same thing when they talk of romances – many sentimental and Gothic novels come between them – she would agree with him that "truth distinguishes our writings from idle romances".

By the time she writes *Camilla* she has decided that the greatest romance of all is the truth – the truth about "the wilder Wonders of the Heart of man; that amazing assemblage of all possible contrarieties". (The reference is to the famous opening lines of Epistle II in Pope's *An Essay on Man*, a poem which Fanny Burney knew well and from which she liked to quote.) But even here, in telling the truth about the human heart, she will "trace nature, yet blot out personality". The word "novel" which she opposed to the perjorative "romance" became itself a term of ill-repute which she did not wish to be used of *Camilla*: "I own I do not like calling it a Novel". This was partly because the word had long delayed the Queen's approval of *Cecilia*. The young princesses had not been allowed to read it until it had been passed by a bishop, and the sales had possibly suffered. But the more important reason is that the word "novel" "gives so simply the notion of a mere love story, that I recoil a little from it. I mean it to be *sketches of Characters and morals, put in action*, not a Romance". Here is the wish (clear again in the phrase "blot out personality") for a more urgent didacticism which marks *Camilla* as a conservative novel of the 1790s. The political and moral climate had changed by 1814 and the debates of the great decade are dead. Mrs Barbauld can write in 1810 of Robert Bage's "democratical" novel *Hermsprong* (1796) that "It was published at a time when sentiments of that nature were prevalent with a large class of people." For Fanny Burney the novel has been further degraded and she wishes *The Wanderer* to be advertised only as "a work: I am passed the time to endure being supposed to write a Love-tale. I will abide by the consequence"; the consequence now being that the sales will suffer if it is *not* called a novel. The work, however, like her three earlier novels will be "a composition upon general life, manners, and characters; without any species of personality"; there is no shift in her opinion that the business of the writer is with the unchanging elements in human nature to be found everywhere from China to Peru. Too much concentration on detail will take away from that general truth which it is the novelist's job to provide, and Fanny Burney refuses to give those details of life in France which her readers had hoped for. Later in the same year *Waverley* offered a whiff of historicism; but Fanny Burney's neo-classicism did not stop her from attempting an historical novel, too, though of a different kind.

As Fanny Burney's distaste for the word "novel" increases, her belief in the thing itself increases too, and her Dedication to *The Wanderer* contains her only defence of fiction. The power of prejudice which attaches to names, she says, is nowhere

> more striking than in the term Novel; a species of writing which, though never mentioned, even by its supporters, but with a look that fears contempt, is not more rigidly excommunicated, from its appelation, in theory, than sought and fostered, from its attractions, in practice.
>
> (*The Wanderer*, I, xx)

But if we can take away for a moment "the title of Novel from its stationary standard of insignificance", we shall find that no form of writing has better opportunities for conveying "useful precepts". Fanny Burney, of course, stresses this didactic function of the novel, which in spite of, or because of (she doesn't make clear which) "an exterior the most frivolous may enwrap illustrations of conduct, that the most rigid preceptor need not deem dangerous to entrust to his pupils".

Thus far her diffidence; now comes her daring. She offers a literary defence and states with her "singular mixture of timidity and confidence" that a novel is perhaps the successor to the Epic; she dares to compare "the compositions which stand foremost, with those which are sunk lowest in literary estimation". It is neither the historical truth nor "the sweet witchery of sound" which gives the epic poem its superiority:

> 'Tis the grandeur, yet singleness of the plan; the never broken, yet never obvious adherence to its execution; the delineation and support of character; the invention of incident; the contrast of situation; the grace of diction, and the beauty of imagery; joined to

a judicious choice of combinations, and a living interest in every partial detail, that give to that sovereign species of the works of fiction, its glorious pre-eminence.

(*The Wanderer*, I, xviii)

The comparison, once made, is a few lines later called futile: all she wished to do was to separate her own work, or fiction ("call it by what name we may") from falsehood; but she had made it. She has made, too, an old-fashioned defence of something new and has said things about *The Wanderer* that could not have been said of *Evelina*.

II

Fanny Burney came to fiction via fact, and the first facts are in the early diary ("Juvenile Journal No. 1", she called it) which she began in March 1768 at the age of sixteen and ten years before the publication of *Evelina*. It is, she says, to be "A Journal in which I must confess my *every* thought, must open my whole heart." It is for her own eyes only, but her instinct is strong for an audience, for a reader or confessor even if it is only an imagined version of herself. She already knows, too, that her flair is for casual, colloquial prose; confession must be like good talk.

> But a thing of this kind ought to be addressed to somebody – I must imagion [*sic*] myself to be talking – talking to the most intimate of friends – to one in whom I should take delight in confiding, and remorse in concealment: – but who must this friend be? to make choice of one in whom I can but *half* rely, would be to frustrate entirely the intention of my plan.

The only satisfactory confidante will be herself, but herself named and dramatized as someone else – "Nobody".

> To Nobody, then, will I write my Journal! since to Nobody can I be wholly unreserved – to Nobody can I reveal every thought, every wish of my heart. . . . No secret *can* I conceal from Nobody, and to Nobody can I be *ever* unreserved.

"Nobody" let her down years later when the elderly Fanny Burney excised many passages from these early diaries; but in the meantime her younger self, having named her reader, addresses every entry to her in the chatty, relaxed prose of uninhibited talk:

> O my dear – such a charming day! and then last night – well, you
> shall have it all in order – as well as I can recollect.
>   Last night . . . Mr Young enter'd the room. O how glad we were
> to see him . . . Hetty sat down to the harpsichord and sung to him
> – mama soon returned and then they left it. *Well, and so* . . .
>   (*ED*, i, 5–7)

A couple of years later the Journal instead of being addressed to Nobody was written either for her sister Susan or for a middle-aged and greatly loved friend of the family, Mr Crisp, who spent much of his time in seclusion some way out of London and who encouraged Fanny Burney to write to him.

What she wrote were journal-letters; that is, letters written over a period of time in the form of a journal and despatched when she found it convenient. It was a form of writing, a genre even, which Fanny Burney was to continue for most of her life, and the first recipients were her sister and Mr Crisp. Since Fanny Burney hoped that Mr Crisp would like what she wrote, there was now an extra need to make the letters lively; confessing every thought and opening one's whole heart was not enough. She was now like her first heroine, Evelina, writing to a much older man whom she saw as another father (she called him "daddy Crisp") whose good opinion she wished for and whose advice she sought, as Evelina sought Mr Villars', and who, like Mr Villars, lived at a distance which made correspondence necessary. She was glad of Mr Crisp's encouragement and she followed his advice on what she should write and how she should write it. The advice was good; the "what" and the "how", he made clear, should be inseparable. She should "dash away whatever comes uppermost" and should clap down on paper "the sudden sallies of imagination". "Stiffness and study" are the worst faults in correspondence, and she must "never think of being correct" when she writes to him. The advice was not only good but necessary, since Fanny Burney inclined even in letters to stiffness, study and a solemn prose at once convoluted and formal which she thought was Johnsonese. In 1775 Mr Crisp is still encouraging her to follow her instinct, still assuring her that "negligence, even incorrectness, now and then in familiar epistolary writing, is the very soul of genius and ease", still warning her against "fine-laboured compositions" that "smelt of the lamp". He did not make her a novelist, but in 1778 the lively journal-letters of Evelina to her guardian show how successful he had been in persuading and guiding her to follow the grain of her genius. Many years later she gave to her son the same advice: "let your pen paint your thoughts as they rise, not as you seek for, or labour to embellish them". A very fine letter from her son, if it had not made her laugh would have made her sick. Frankness is everything, and Alex is urged to let his pen "run on in letters without either study or circumspection". Because she wrote like this herself in letters which were praised and enjoyed by all her correspondents ("You have learned to make your descriptions live", Mr Crisp told her) she naturally cast her first novel in letter form and made of it, in effect, her longest journal-letter. *Evelina* is successful because its letters, "written from the thoughts that occur to the Pen at the moment", are successful, and because in it the art of the journal-letter and the art of the novel are the same thing.

Fanny Burney came to fiction via fact: her journals precede her fiction. But what is fact and what is fiction? *Which* is fact and *which* is fiction? The novels as well as the journals depend upon memory, and Fanny Burney's memory was remarkable; but the very resemblance in style and form of these first journals to Evelina's letters to her guardian raises questions. Memory means many things. It is not simply the power of recall, but it can include total or substantial recall of what was actually said on a particular occasion. Fanny Burney was present at the opening of the Warren Hastings trial in 1788 and records in a journal-letter to her sister Susan the opening statement (about 150 words) of the Chancellor, Lord Thurlow. She does not here claim complete accuracy; however, "I will give it you to the best of my power from memory; the newspapers have printed it far less accurately than I have retained it."[4] It is not possible to verify her account since it is precisely the potential verifiers (the newspapers) which cannot be trusted. Her accounts of conversations were never disputed, and she gave the same gift to Evelina who transcribes a conversation four hundred words long and related "in a hasty manner" between Mrs Selwyn and Sir John Belmont; "yet I believe I can recollect every word". The total recall of the omniscient author is no longer a literary convention.

Memory can sometimes be lost in imagination. In her "Ilfracombe Journal", written sixteen years after the event, Fanny Burney tells how in the late summer of 1817 she went with her dog for a walk on the beach at Ilfracombe. After spending some time exploring the rocks and caverns, she found that her return was cut off by the tide and she was forced to find safety from the sea by climbing to the top of a pinnacle where a small patch of grass provided a sort of seat. The six hours of waiting terror before she was discovered by her son and his friend are dramatically described, as is the further fear of being molested by escaped Irish rebels who (she believed) had sought refuge in the caves on the north Devon coast. The episode is a vivid one; but years later when her rescuer's son read the account of it his comments were dismissive and dry:

> The lady's account of her adventure was greatly exaggerated – She was in no real danger – The sea had not come up to her. She was not clinging to the rocks – She was seated on the sand. The incident of the little dog . . . was an invention as far as my father recollected – He could not be said to have saved her life but his happy suggestion that she might have been caught by the tide saved her from enough inconvenience.
>
> (*Journals*, x, 714n)

This particular journal is unusual in recounting a series of events most of which could not be verified and in containing almost no dialogue; for above all else it is dialogue and the accompanying gestures, looks and tones of voice which Fanny Burney is keen to note and which are the most astonishing features of all her journals. Her distinguished editor and biographer (Joyce Hemlow) says that "in her eighteenth year Fanny had learned to record direct speech, even long conversations, an art by no means easy";[5] but this explains very little, and the comment that "she had a memory like a tape-recorder, a mind like a *camera obscura*", explains even less. This is a too simple and therefore a false view of how memory works. Fanny Burney never claimed such accuracy. Even when at the age of thirty-six she noted Lord Thurlow's address at the trial of Warren Hastings and would have wanted such accuracy she is "by no means exact or secure". A tape-recording of nearly every casual conversation would be enormously boring, and Fanny Burney is never that; and, in any case, she accompanies the words with looks and gestures. To speak of the accurate recording of long conversations as an art is misleading. It is a skill: the art lies in the selection, compression and dramatic shaping of the words said. It has never been suggested that Fanny Burney somehow made miraculous transcripts of every spoken word and then later edited and shortened the conversations by omission and emphasis. In a letter to Mr Crisp in 1774 she says of a social scene, "I shall recollect as much of the conversation as I can, and make the parties speak for themselves."[6] She then gives the talk of six people as if it were a scene from a play with the speakers named on the side of the page. It is a sparkling two minutes of chat (the time it takes to read it) but it gives the impression of being very much longer. There are no hesitations, no irrelevancies, and all the contributions are shaped and dove-tail easily. Total accuracy is not the same thing as total recall, and a short extract will give the flavour and show the skill of the young Fanny Burney's art. (The opening references are to Dr Burney's second marriage in 1767.)

Miss Reid. – You was saying, Mrs Brooke, that you did not know till I told you that Dr Burney had a wife; what do you think then of seeing these grown up daughters?

Mrs Brooke. – Why, I don't know, [or why,] but I own I was never more surprised than when I heard that Dr Burney was married.

Dr Shebbeare. – What, I suppose you did not take him for a fool? – All men who marry are so, but above all God help him who takes a widow!

Mr Strange. – This is a strange man, Mrs Burney, but nobody ever minds him.

Dr Shebbeare. – I don't wonder that Dr Burney went abroad! – all my amazement is at his ever coming home! unless, indeed, he left his understanding behind him, which I suppose was the case.

Mrs Brooke. – I am sure that does not appear from his Tour. I never received more pleasure than from reading his account of what he saw and did abroad.

Dr Shebbeare. – I hate authors! but I suppose one wit must hate another.

Mrs Brooke. – Those few authors that *I* know give me great reason not to hate them; – quite the contrary – Dr Johnson, Dr Armstrong, and I wont say *what* I think of Dr Burney; but for Dr Armstrong I have a very particular regard. I have known him more than twenty years.

Dr Shebbeare. – What, I suppose you like him for his intrigues?

Mrs Brooke. – Indeed, I never heard he had any.

Dr Shebbeare. – What, I suppose you had too many yourself to keep his in your memory?

Mrs Brooke. – O, women, you know, Dr, never have intrigues. I wish Dr Burney was here, I am sure he would be our champion.

Dr Shebbeare. – What, do you suppose he'd speak against himself? I know but too well what it is to be married! I think I have been yoked for one and forty years, and I have wished my wife under ground any time since.

Mama. – And if she were you'd marry in a week!

Dr Shebbeare. – I wish I was tried.

Mr Strange. – Why this is a sad man, Mrs Burney, I think we must toss him in a blanket.

Dr Shebbeare. – Ay, with all my heart. But speak for yourself (to Mrs Brooke), do you suppose your husband was not long since tired of you?

Mrs Brooke. – O, as to that – that is not a fair question; – I don't ask you if you're tired of *your* wife.

Dr Shebbeare. – And if you did, I'd tell you.

Miss Beatson. – Then *I* ask you, Dr Shebbeare, are you tired of your wife?

Dr Shebbeare. – I did not say I'd tell *you*, Bold Face.

Mama. – I wish that Mrs Strange was here; she'd fight our battles admirably.

Mr Strange. – Why do you never come to see her, Doctor?

Dr Shebbeare. – Because she has so much tongue, that I expect she'll talk herself to death, and I don't choose to be accessary.

(*ED*, I, 286–7)

The mere naming of the speakers and the recording of their talk without comment is a method that Boswell characteristically uses; and it is Boswell, whom Fanny Burney knew and for whom she felt an irritated liking, who is closest to her gifts and method.

In a fine essay, "The Power of Memory in Boswell and Scott", F. A. Pottle[7] indirectly helps us to understand the art of Fanny Burney's journals and the nature of the memory revealed in them. Boswell, he claims, had "something that looks like total recall", but he needed to make some notes, however brief, soon after the event in order to achieve this recall at a later period. His notes for his journals or for his *Life of Johnson* are fragmentary, even obscure, and there is no hint in them of any selection or emphasis. The finished product, if written up only a few hours later or as much as fourteen

years later, was very different. Dr Johnson himself was quite aware
that what Boswell was doing was not transcript, but art. In his
Journal of a Tour to the Hebrides Boswell writes in his entry for the 19th
of September (1773):

> He [Dr Johnson] came to my room this morning before breakfast,
> to read my Journal, which he has done all along. He often before
> said, 'I take great delight in reading it'. To-day he said, 'You
> improve: it grows better and better.' – I observed, there was a
> danger of my getting a habit of writing in a slovenly manner. –
> 'Sir, said he, it is not written in a slovenly manner. It might be
> printed, were the subject fit for printing.'

Johnson's delight is not in the comprehensive ramblings of a
tape-recorder; and what grew better and better was obviously not
Boswell's total recall (the recorded conversations for the previous
day which Johnson had just read may be read in two minutes) but
his creative selectivity.

In Fanny Burney's journals and journal-letters, in Boswell's
journals and *Life of Johnson*, the lapse of time between the events and
their writing-up could vary from a few hours to many years. She,
too, (like Boswell) compiled her journals from notes. Joyce Hemlow
quotes from a diary MS for August 1786: "I shall now begin a new
pacquet from my Pocket Book memorandums, which are minutely
faithful, and which I set down every morning from the events of the
preceding Day." And again in 1788 she writes: "I write every
morning at Breakfast memorandums of the preceding Day, which I
keep by me, till I have opportunity to draw them out intelligibly."[8]
As with Boswell a short note was enough for a later large-scale
recollection; without it (and the distinction is hers) she must rely on
mere *memory*. "This little had I written before Christmas – and now,
3 months after, I must have recourse to my memory – For
memorandums I have none, for endeavouring to recollect what I
meant to relate."[9] Without a brief note she could bring back nothing.
Writing to her sister about the opening of Warren Hastings' trial she
says: "The interest of this trial was so much upon my mind, that I
have not kept even a memorandum of what passed from the 13th of
February to the day when I went again to Westminster Hall; nor . . .
do I recollect one circumstance."[10] Later she finds it nearly
impossible to write her diary for November of the same year.
"November. – This month will be very brief of annals; I was so ill, so

unsettled, so unhappy during every day that I kept not a memorandum."[11] In Boswell and Fanny Burney we sometimes have two versions of the same episode or conversation; an account written close to the event and a second one years later. In Boswell's case, however, the second version is seldom an expansion of the first but is more usually a compression of it. Fanny Burney's later versions in journal form are usually much longer and much more circumstantial than the earlier ones in letters.

Joyce Hemlow has shown how Fanny Burney's journals and journal-letters were "constructed" weeks, months or even many years after the events narrated. The early journals were often written to a confidante, her sister Susan, and have therefore a frankness that was impossible in later journals after her move to France in 1802, by which time her sister was dead and there was no-one to take her place. Joyce Hemlow calls these later journals "semi-literary productions, composed from letters, memoranda, and recourse to memory, years, sometimes six to twelve years, after the event".[12] Memory, then, in these journals is of two different kinds. There is the memory which made possible the earlier account in a letter, itself an ordered selection; and then imposed upon it is a memory which up to twelve years later could still call upon other previously unrecorded memories and so extend the original memory, improve it in dramatic quality and, most curiously, add circumstantial, convincing detail. The term "semi-literary" does nothing to explain Fanny Burney's remarkable memory. It cannot mean semi-fictional, for the basis of the longer accounts is in earlier written accounts; and it cannot mean more vivid, for sometimes the earlier versions are best. It can only mean more imaginative, but not, of course, more imaginary. In a letter written from Brussels to her husband on the 15 and 18 June (the day of Waterloo) she gives a brief but intense picture of the panic that has seized the city and herself and of the sounds and rumours of war. All day on the 18 June contradictory stories came from the battlefield and no certain news of victory reached Brussels until evening. In her letter Fanny Burney tells her husband that "I shall set out to-morrow morning, at 5 o'clock, If Danger here approaches with the family of the Boyds, for Antwerp. (Anvers.)." Much later in the day she adds to the same letter, "I am come therefore, to the Boyds, to be in readiness for departing for Anvers to-morrow . . .". In "The Waterloo Journal" written eight years later in 1823 the story of how she came to the Boyds is expanded from seven words ('I am come therefore, to the

Boyds") to seven pages. A false alarm was given in the late afternoon that the French army was entering Brussels.

> I know not even who made this declaration: my head was out of the Window, &, in drawing it in, I heard it; but the person who made it scarcely entered the room & was gone; leaving the door wide open, & running down stairs; or perhaps up; for my alarm was too great for observation; & a general sense of being struck with indecorum, or even hurry, for the first time in that house, encreased my conviction of danger.
>
> How terrific was this moment! the most so, perhaps, for its immediate horrour, of my Life – though not, alas, the most afflicting! – Oh no! – but while my Imagination rushed into Dungeons, Prisons, pillage, Insult, bloodshed, mangled carcases, Fire, & murder, my recollection failed me not, & my perilous situation; if surprized in Apartments belonging to an Officer of the body Guard of Louis 18, then in active service for that Monarch, urged me to instant flight; &, without waiting to speak to the people of the house, I crammed my Letters, papers, & money into a straw flat Basket, given my by my beloved Friend Mrs Lock, & throwing on a Shawl & Bonnet, I flew down stairs & out of doors.
>
> (*Journals*, VIII, 439)

"My intention," she continues, "was to go to the Boyds" and the details of her going take five more pages. It is the unverifiable, circumstantial and unimportant detail of the "straw flat basket", remembered after all those years but not mentioned in any earlier account, which convinces us of the scene's truthfulness and of the reality of her own emotional response; this, and the collapsed syntax in the second paragraph and the paradoxical recall of the detail she does not remember – whether the person who had given the alarm about the French had run upstairs or down.

Boswell is not concerned with things like this. He may sometimes suffer chagrin at things Dr Johnson says to him, and if this chagrin is great enough he simply suppresses what was said; but the chagrin or any other emotion is offered as a fact and not dramatized as an experience. In the *Life* he has no interest in his own or Johnson's emotional life, and the circumstantial details are always literally that: details of the circumstances such as dates and places and never the pointless but important memory of insignificant things like a straw basket. Boswell did not, in any case, have to remember dates and places; he either noted them at the time or, when necessary, researched them years later. His supreme gift, like Fanny Burney's, was for remembering the spoken word; and her conversations, like Boswell's, are neither complete records nor imaginary constructions. What they are is something different: imaginative treatment of the truth by selection, emphasis, circumstantial (and theoretically verifiable) detail, all made possibly by an absorbed attention. Boswell was all attention to Dr Johnson's words; Fanny Burney was always listening and watching, always from an early age "the silent observant Miss Fanny".[13] Boswell was impressed by that "stretch of mind" which enabled him to bring back lengthy conversations; but he knew that more was needed. In July 1763, two months after meeting Johnson, Boswell apologizes for his early imperfect record of Johnson's talk and explains his gradual improvement:

> In the early part of my acquaintance with him . . . I found it extremely difficult to recollect and record his conversation with its genuine vigour and vivacity. In progress of time when my mind was, as it were, *strongly impregnated with the Johnsonian ether*, I could with more facility and exactness, carry in my memory and commit to paper the exuberant variety of his wisdom and wit.

This is wittily expressed but is not quite the whole truth since Boswell could also remember the words spoken by other members of Dr Johnson's circle, and since what he finally put on paper was a very heavily selective reconstruction (based on a few notes) of what was actually said.

In 1791 Fanny Burney gave regular accounts of the Warren Hastings trial to the King and Queen.

> When we came home I was immediately summoned to Her Majesty, to whom I gave a full and fair account of all I had heard of the defence; and it drew tears from her expressive eyes, as I repeated Mr. Hasting's own words, upon the hardship and injustice of the treatment he had sustained.
>
> Afterwards, at night, the King called upon me to repeat my account; and I was equally faithful, sparing nothing of what had dropped from the persecuted defendant relative to His Majesty's Ministers. I thought official accounts might be less detailed there

than against the Managers, who, as open enemies, excite not so much my "high displeasure" as friends of Government . . .

The King listened with much earnestness and a marked compassion. He had already read the account sent him officially, but he was as eager to hear all I could recollect, as if still uninformed of what had passed. The words may be given to the eye, but the impression they make can only be conveyed by the ear; and I came back so eagerly interested, that my memory was not more stored with the very words than my voice with the intonations of all that had passed.

(Diary, v, 168–9).

It was Fanny Burney's attention ("eagerly interested") which made possible the extensive, but still selective, reporting of the trial. But she is more ambitious than Boswell in attempting to recover for the King, as she does for her correspondent in her written account, not merely the words that were spoken but the very "intonations" of all that had passed. Boswell and Fanny Burney tried to recover extended conversations, but his accounts are much shorter than hers; even a long evening's talk at the club seldom extends beyond two pages. When Fanny Burney has reported Lord Thurlow's speech she gives an account of several conversations while the various charges against Warren Hastings were being read in "so monotonous a chant" that she could scarcely hear or understand anything. During these undramatic formalities she chatted briefly with people sitting near her, and at greater length with William Wyndham whom she was willing to like because of his earlier kindness to Dr Johnson, but who had now vexed her by appearing as one of the principal prosecutors of Warren Hastings. The first of these dialogues with Wyndham covers thirteen pages and the second about seven. It is, of course, very difficult to estimate how long in real time the two conversations lasted, but ten or fifteen minutes would be a reasonable guess. The contrast with Boswell's two or three pages for three hours is striking; Fanny Burney's account is fuller, and because the original conversations were shorter her selection is less severe and less obvious.

There is, however, another reason for these longer accounts: Fanny Burney recalls not simply the words but the looks and gestures of the speakers, the "intonations' of the words and descriptions of her own feelings. Many years earlier she reported a conversation as if it were a scene from a play; now she reports conversations as if they were scenes from a novel. In Boswell's *Life* the drama is in the words and the wit and the argument, and only seldom (as in the famous meeting with Wilkes) in the situation or the clash of personalities. Certainly in the record of her conversations with Wyndham (and with many others) Fanny Burney emerges as an agile talker, but the interest and drama comprehended more than the words. The trial itself was a dramatic event. When she saw the former Governor-General "cast at the feet of his enemies" (formalities required that he should kneel briefly at the bar) she could scarcely keep herself from running from Westminster Hall. But that was only the public drama and there were other small, private dramas. First of all Hastings was a family friend who was now being attacked by other family friends, Sheridan, Wyndham and, above all, Burke: "How did I grieve to behold him now the cruel Prosecutor (such to me he appeared) of an injured and innocent man!" Then there were little dramas of embarrassment. She was embarrassed in case Hastings might notice her talking to Wyndham and suspect that her sympathies lay with the opposition. There was the even greater embarrassment of being noticed at all in a public place. Sir Joshua Reynolds, an old friend but also an opponent of Hastings, insisted on bowing and smiling and nodding to her, "making at the same time a sign to his ear, by which I understood he had no trumpet". (He was deaf.) There were dramas of possible misunderstandings. Because of Fanny Burney's position at court it was assumed that she always supported court opinion, and that this explained her defence of Hastings since he had the support of the King and Queen. The Queen herself was present on the first day of the trial and could see Fanny Burney in a "close and eager conference with an avowed member of opposition" which would cause "conjectures innumerable" and would later have to be explained and excused. Embarrassment and fear of misunderstandings are the staple of her first novels, and by this year (1788), with two successful novels published, the desire to release the novelist from the pages of the journal writer is so strong that she more than half assumes the role of omniscient author.

> I soon saw Mr Wyndham harboured no personal rancour: he was a stranger to the very person of Mr Hastings, and wholly ignorant of his character in private and social life. I was happy in those points to be permitted to give him some intelligence, and I saw by the surprise with which he listened that he had imagined Mr

Hastings as mean in his parts, and as disagreeable in his manners, as he believes him to be cruel in his nature and worthless in his principles.

(*Diary*, IV, 68)

Not only an omniscient author but an all-seeing one. Fanny Burney comments that Lord Thurlow's speech was "uttered in a calm, equal, solemn manner, and in a voice mellow and penetrating, with eyes keen and black, yet softened into some degree of tenderness".[14] The manner and voice we may accept; but when we remember that Fanny Burney was seated at one end of Westminster Hall and that the Lord Chancellor spoke from the middle of the hall, it is clear that the description of his eyes and their expression must be, if not quite fiction, interpretation.

The chief interest of the scene is in the character of William Wyndham as it emerges from his talk with Fanny Burney and from her author-like commentary and analysis. We may feel a simple sorrow for Hamlet's father, but our interest is in his son; Fanny Burney's sadness was all for Hastings, but the novelist's attention caught the drama in the prosecutor Wyndham. Hastings was not able to speak to her, but conversation was possible with Wyndham and this gave her the chance to write one of the finest long passages in her journal-letters. She had no interest in the state of Denmark – no interest, that is, in the politics of the trial or the reasons for it. Because she was certain of Hastings's simple innocence he could not engage her deepest interest. But Wyndham could. Here was a man whom she liked but who was on the wrong side in the trial; someone whose humanity and generous spirit were at war with his party spirit; someone who interested her and whom she hoped to convert. This interest and hope shape the scene which begins with (in Fanny Burney's eyes) Wyndham's unthinking, unfeeling assumption of Hasting's guilt, moves to his growing sensibility, even dismay, and then to her growing conviction (based on intonation and gesture as much as words) that Wyndham considered Hastings innocent and could only with self-laceration continue the prosecution.

The longest reported exchanges with Wyndham are those which suggest his increasing uncertainty and perplexity as Fanny Burney's discreet conviction of Hastings's innocence and his own imaginative sympathy clash with his political belief in Hastings's guilt. He is impressed by the greatness of Hastings' fall:

"Wonderful indeed! almost past credibility, is such a reverse! He that, so lately, had the Eastern World nearly at his beck; he, under whose tyrant power princes and potentates sunk and trembled; he, whose authority was without the reach of responsibility! –"

Again he stopped, seeming stuck, almost beyond the power of speech, with meditative commiseration . . .

(*Diary*, IV, 57)

In this sudden hesitation Wyndham reminds Fanny Burney of Hamlet. But, she continues, he suddenly roused himself "as if recollecting his 'almost blighted purpose' ". In the second conversation she notes a change: "I saw he was much agitated; the gaiety which seems natural to him was flown, and had left in its place the most evident and unquiet emotion", which she now dramatizes in his reflections to her and interprets in her comments – she decides that the smile is "half-conscious":

"This day – for which we have all been waiting so anxiously, so earnestly – now that it is actually arrived, it takes me as if I had never thought of it before – it comes upon me all unexpected, and finds me unready!"

Still I said nothing, for I did not fully comprehend him, till he added, "I will not be so affected as to say to you that I have made no preparation – that I have not thought a little upon what I have to do; yet now that the moment is actually come –"

(*Diary*, IV, 70–1)

She notes Wyndham's generous sympathy and his hesitations, and she is again reminded of Hamlet's hesitations and of his father's injunction to remember:

He was affected too, himself; but presently, rising, he said with great quickness, "I must shake all this off; I must have done with it – dismiss it – forget that he is there."

"O, no," cried I, earnestly, "do not forget it!"

"Yes, yes; I must."

"No, *remember* it rather," cried I; "I could almost (putting up my hands as if praying) do thus; and then, like poor Mr. Hastings just now to the house, drop down on my knees to you, to call out *'Remember it.'* "

"Yes, yes," cried he, precipitately, "how else shall I go on? I *must* forget that *He* is there, and that *you* are here."
And then he hurried down to his Committee.
Was it not a most singular scene?

(*Diary*, IV, 76)

All selective reporting of conversation, even Boswell's of Johnson, is inevitably interpretation, but Fanny Burney in this "scene" (her word) goes much further. We seldom want to call Boswell's report of an evening's talk a "scene". His interpretations are unconscious; Fanny Burney's are the deliberate selection of an artist sensing the dramas in an episode and shaping them to a specific end. Or ends. In her talk with Wyndham she does what she can for Hastings; in her account to the Queen she does what she can to change the unfavourable Royal opinion of Wyndham. "So candid, so liberal is the mind of the Queen, that she not only heard me with the most favourable attention towards Mr Wyndham, but was herself touched even to tears by the relation."[15] Her art persuades; and her art is her memory for circumstantial detail and for the imaginative reconstruction and interpretation of talk.

The details are not simply of time and place, or small gestures or dress and appearance; they can be much more surprising and therefore persuasive. She enriches her memory of a past episode by remembering herself remembering. As she sits in Westminster Hall she hears someone speak to her: "I turned about and saw Mr Crutchley. All Streatham rose to my mind at sight of him. I have never beheld him since the Streatham society was abolished. We entered instantly upon the subject of that family."[16] A little later she learns from her brother Charles that Wyndham, whom she had not met for some time, wished to be introduced to her. Time, place and circumstance make her want to avoid the meeting; but she remembers that "He loved Dr Johnson – and Dr Johnson returned his affection", and she recalls that when he heard that Dr Johnson was taken ill on his last visit to Lichfield, he set off from London in his own carriage "to offer to bring him back to town in it, and at his own time".[17] So memory comes in aid of memory and (in Wordsworth's phrase) "feeling comes in aid of feeling" to create a densely remembered and emotionally complex episode.

Sometimes she draws attention to her own power of memory for small detail. She confesses to Wyndham that since she is equally the admirer of Hastings and of his chief prosecutor, Burke, she scarcely knows any more what she wishes. Wyndham assures her that all her doubts will soon be decided:

> "That doubt is, of all states the worse: it will soon, however, be over; you must be all one way the moment you have heard Burke."
> "I am not quite so sure of that!" cried I, boldly.
> "No?" cried he, looking amazed at me.
> "No, indeed! But if it seems strange to you that I should own this, you must impute it all to the want of that malignity which I cannot see in you!"
> The odd civility of this speech, which was a literal truth, again brought back his gaiety . . .
>
> (*Diary*, IV, 72)

The "odd civility" persuades us that it is accurately remembered and gives to the talk a curious emotional colouring. Remembered detail in Fanny Burney is never random and separate but gives to each episode shape, significance and emotional unity.

In his *Life of Johnson* Boswell gives interest to an evening's conversation by intense selection and compression. (Dr Johnson's talk is more interesting in Boswell's *Life* than in Fanny Burney's journals.) Fanny Burney interests by expansion, conscious interpretation and a steady search for significance. Boswell's interpretations are unconscious; they move, remarks Pottle "on the plane of average or normal experience, with the result that in him we seem to see the past through no kind of medium at all", and he contrasts this with the much more common medium "which colours or distorts".[18] His contrast is with Carlyle and Scott; but Fanny Burney, who colours but does not distort, is a more interesting contrast. All things are coloured by her consciousness, by her ability to find drama in a straw, by her willingness to create it where she does not find it, and by her imaginings of fear, embarrassment and disaster. She was a novelist whose letters and journals tend towards novel but not towards fiction. In the eccentric, wayward, posturing, romantic Boswell there was nothing of the novelist; in the *Life* he was exclusively interested in Johnson and in his journals he was fascinated only by himself. In the *Life* people are so many lights to illuminate Dr Johnson's wisdom and wit, and events and anecdotes are so many different angles from which to view him; in Boswell's journals everything is food for his own insatiable, marvellous display of self. Pottle shows that when Walter Scott recalls places or anecdotes or snatches of conversation his "imaginative construction is at work . . . in the same way" as in his novels and permits him to "remember" things he could never have seen. (It is only in his own great *Journal*, intended for no reader, that the novelist is at rest and Scott affects us by the literalness and bareness of his narration.) Fanny Burney with her eye for detail convinces us (as Boswell does) that what she records actually happened; and it can never be shown (as it can with Scott) that certain things could not have happened, could not have been seen, could not have been heard. Yet her imagination is as consciously at work in her journals and letters as in her novels, and in the same way. Conversations in the journals are as long as conversations in the novels. The twelve pages that record her first conversation wtih Wyndham at the Hastings trial are not a triumph of memory but a triumph of an art which her first two novels had formed and fostered. Her memory was, of course, remarkable but could not itself create the interest of such dialogue as this; and however remarkable her memory, it is not possible to believe that the hundreds of pages of dialogue in her journals are a transcript of what was said. She never pretended they were. Several times she gives two accounts of the same scene with omissions, additions and alterations. For example in *The Early Diary* she describes a small concert given by her father in honour of Prince Orloff,[19] and though many phrases are repeated, many are changed. Lady Edgecumbe's comments on the singers are not only altered but are redistributed to other points of the conversation. In a journal-letter of 1786 she quotes the immensely boring chat of a Colonel Goldsmith:

> "I vow, ma'am," cried the Colonel, "I would not have taken such a liberty on any account; though all the comfort of my life, in this house, is one half-hour in a day spent in this room. After all one's labours, riding, and walking, and standing, and bowing – what a life it is? Well! it's honour! that's one comfort; it's all honour! royal honour! – one has the honour to stand till one has not a foot left; and to ride till one's stiff, and to walk till one's ready to drop, – and then one makes one's lowest bow, d'ye see, and blesses one's self with joy for the honour!"
> This is his style of rattle, when perfectly at his ease . . .
> (*Diary*, III, 151)

Fanny Burney could not have remembered word for word even this short extract from the pages of similar trivia that follow. Her comment on the colonel's talk – "This is his kind of rattle" – shows that she is giving an impressionistic and not literal account of his monologue and is trying to reveal his character (or absence of character) through the triviality of his talk. (This is a method she uses in her novels.) The conversations with Wyndham show a more sophisticated art, but one not intended to deceive. Words, looks, gestures, tones of voice are given in a rich detail which we cannot believe to be factual recall, and are interpreted with the authority of a novelist and not by herself as participant. When she says, for example, in her report that he "paused expressively" or that he gave a "conscious look" she knows as omniscient author what the pause expresses and of what the look is conscious. There can be no other interpretations than the ones she gives; even in retrospect she shows no uncertainty or doubt, no acknowledgement that she could be wrong. And when she says in the passage quoted earlier that "the odd civility of this speech . . . again brought back his gaiety", she is seeing – creating – cause and effect and thus giving interest, shape and finally truth and conviction to the whole creatively remembered scene.

Fanny Burney, in spite of herself, liked Boswell but did not think highly of his *Life of Johnson* or of his way of writing it. Some years before its publication she called Boswell a "biographical anecdotical memorandummer" and some years after its publication she condemned "his loquacious communications of every weakness and infirmity of the first and greatest good man of these times". She pays no tribute to Boswell's memory or power of selection. She does not doubt the accuracy and truth of what he says, but questions the propriety of saying it. "Anecdote" and "memorandum" are for Fanny Burney belittling terms; a memorandum (that is, a short note) was for her the mere spark which days, weeks, months, years would fan into flame. There is, of course, in her journals nothing of the Romantic mode of memory. We do not ask if Wordsworth's memories are accurate: the question has no meaning. Nor have the memories; they are simply of vast importance to the poet. The facts are nothing: their significance and interpretation are everything. Fanny Burney is closer to Boswell. Unlike him she recalls with the genius of a novelist; like him she remembers within the limits of literal, verifiable circumstance.

III

Fanny Burney's journals, diaries and letters are literary productions. The Editor of *The Early Diary*, Annie Raine Ellis, wants to distinguish the letters from the journals and to find in the former the materials for the latter. She refers to Fanny Burney's six to twelve quarto page letters to Mr Crisp: "In these she described scenes while they were still vivid before her eyes, or reported conversations which were almost sounding in her ears."[20] These letters are then contrasted with the corresponding accounts in her journal which are rightly called

> often *retrospective*, being written as she could snatch time, at some distance from the events. They are perhaps a little more orderly in arrangement of speeches, and incidents than the letters; otherwise they differ very little. Now and then, the letters have details which are omitted in the journal, and *vice versa*; but the difference is not considerable.
>
> (*ED*, II, 1)

The attempt to make distinctions, however slight, between letters and journals is unconvincing; and a qualifying phrase like "perhaps a little more orderly" hints that the editor is not herself convinced. Her letters (and not only those to Mr Crisp) were themselves retrospective, and were "worked-up" (Fanny Burney's phrase) from memoranda or notes which she had made at a point still nearer to the event. (None of these notes has survived.) In 1802 her father urged her to "make Memorandums of all you hear and see", and in her letter of reply she says she can only guide him to the details "by having recourse to my original *notes*, kept entirely for my dearest Padre, and from then I will prepare him such food . . .". All writing, including notes, is retrospective; her letters and journals, however close to the event, were equally recreated through recourse to notes, and "the artistry of pattern is almost as manifest in [them] as in fiction".[21]

The novels (and not simply *Evelina*) emerge from her autobiographical writings – from the letters and diaries and journals where, as John Butt says, "the essential material of her fiction is to be found in plenty".[22] There are, however, different kinds of essential material, many of them not in any way direct transfers of experience; and some of the most dramatic episodes in her life, such as her meeting with the deranged George III in Kew Gardens, appear nowhere in her novels. Fanny Burney would have thought such an episode too implausible and to untypical in its specific circumstances to be of use to her in charting the fears and embarrassments of a young woman making her first "entrance into the world".

The connections between her diaries and her fiction can often be simple and obvious. Some of the characters in her letters and diaries reappear in her novels. A certain Dr King whose "exaggerated praises of England" are recorded in a conversation with a Russian called Pogenpohl in her diary for 1772 is probably the source of the vulgar, chauvinistic Captain Mirvan in *Evelina*.

> "Our universities, Sir," said he, "are the only schools in Europe for learning; they bring forth geniuses superior to all the world."
> "Are they, then," said the Russian archly, "all geniuses, Sir?"
> "They are the noblest schools in the world," said the Doctor.
> "You think them superior to *all* others, Sir?" cried Mr Pogenpohl, naming some one which I have forgot.
> "Undoubtedly, Sir. What nation has brought forth such men as our's? Have we not Lock?"
> "Oh, oui! and you have Newton! but then have we not Volfe (*sic*) and Beraman (*sic*), – was not he the father of Civil Law? Who have you, Sirs, in that class?"
> "Why, as to that –" said the Doctor.
> "As to that," repeated Mr. Lattice, – "I can't say."
> "But, Sir," continued the Doctor with a vehemence, which, rude as it was, was merely put on, to give himself imaginary consequence, "but, Sir, are we not superior to all the world in Astronomy? in Natural History? in Poetry? in Philosophy? in Music?"
>
> (*ED*, i, 155)

The editing and control (and therefore comedy) of this scene are more impressive than similar ones with Captain Mirvan, and the element of crude Smollettian farce is absent. The "philanthropic ramblings" of a certain Mr Hutton in 1774 are one probable source for the character of Albany in *Cecilia*. Fanny Burney's brother Charles whose "light-hearted gaiety savoured, the family thought, of levity" is a model for "the candidate for every order of whim, the light-hearted mirthful Lionel" in *Camilla*. The dread Mrs

Schwellenberg, Keeper of the Robes to Queen Charlotte, and Fanny
Burney's superior at court, was a model for the "gloomy, dark,
suspicious, rude, reproachful" Mrs Ireton in *The Wanderer* and for
the governess Miss Margland in *Camilla* "whose disposition was so
querulous, that, in her constant suspicion of humiliation, she
seemed always looking for an affront, and ready primed for a
contest". Source-hunting of this kind is usually an empty exercise in
trivial ingenuity; but in going from a character in the journals or
letters to a character in the novels we are not in a simple way going
from the fact to the fiction, from someone real to someone
imaginary. What the comparisons reveal is a later portrait modifying
an earlier portrait, one artistic creation growing out of another,
imagination building upon imagination.

    More interesting are the many parallels between the stiuations in
which Fanny Burney finds herself in the journals and the situations
of her heroines. In 1780, for example, at a public breakfast in the
Spring Gardens in Bath, Fanny Burney found herself talking to a
young woman, Miss W—, of a gloomy and misanthropic cast of
mind, who announced that she was miserable at home, that all men
were bad ("all sensualists") and that the only happiness would be to
meet someone as extravagant in sentiments as herself. Fanny
Burney "stared much at a severity of speech for which her softness
of manner had so ill prepared me", and stared even harder – was
"quite thunderstruck" – when Miss W—explained that all happiness
in this world was impossible and that she would not hesitate
a moment "to put a violent end" to her life. Fanny Burney
investigates and argues. Hume, it seems, is the cause of Miss W—'s
infidelity and despair, and Fanny Burney in half a dozen lines
crisply recommends as antidotes the Bible, "Beattie on the
Immutability of Truth" and the poet Mason's "Elegy on Lady
Coventry".[23] A young woman "in a very dangerous situation, with
ideas so loose of religion, and so enthusiastic of love" appears
thirty-four years later in *The Wanderer* as Elinor, who tries to commit
suicide twice and is dissuaded by the hero from a third attempt only
after a sermon of thirty pages on immortality.[24] In 1788 during the
first attack of the King's illness Fanny Burney describes in some
excellent pages the sense of dread and impending disaster at
Windsor, the whisperings, the silences and the stillness in the small
hours of the rooms and corridors at the Lodge. " 'Tis too interesting
ever to escape my own memory", she says in a journal-letter; and
many years later in *Camilla* the remembered silence at Windsor and

the premonition of disaster create the unease of the heroine's entry into her uncle's empty house at Cleves.[25] In 1773 Fanny Burney tells how she suffered the teasing, ambiguous attentions of an elderly man, Mr Crispen; she does not know if he spoke in sport when he asked her for kisses, but she catches the silly whimsy of his manner of speaking to her:

> We returned first, and were just seated, when we heard a rap at the parlour door. "Come in," cried I, "whoever you are." The door opened and Mr Crispen entered. "Whose sweet voice bid me come in?" cried he, "May I hope that my love welcomes me?" He came immediately and drew a chair before me, as I sat on the window, and began to relate his sufferings from his long absence.
>
> (*ED*, I, 253)

Mr Crispen becomes "somewhat troublesome in taking, or rather making, perpetual opportunities of taking my hand". Fanny Burney's growing embarrassment and vexation are recalled (though not more effectively presented) in *The Wanderer* when the heroine is confused and embarrassed by the attentions of "the gouty old Baronet", Sir Jaspar Herrington, who speaks with all the vapid facetiousness of Mr Crispen. Juliet asks if she may make a request: "Request?" repeated Sir Jaspar . . . "Can you utter any thing but commands? The most benignant sprite of all Fairyland, has inspired you with this gracious disposition to dub me your knight."[26] In 1770, after a supper party at a Mrs Pringle's, a proposal is made to rehearse and perform a play – a farce by Garrick called *Miss in Her Teens*. Fanny Burney (still in her teens) is embarrassed when she reads it and finds the part of Tag which she was to play "quite shocking – indeed I would not have done it for the universe". She finds support for her refusal from Mrs Pringle (as Fanny Price does from Mary Crawford) who read the play "attentively" and said to her sons "she was sure I should not do it". This remembered confusion is used briefly in *Camilla* and again in *The Wanderer* when Juliet is reluctant even to prompt in a play.

These (and many other) specific parallels, however, matter less than the endless embarrassment and constant fear of shame which colour the diaries and are the very atmosphere of the novels. There are, of course, what Jane Austen calls "the little zig-zags of embarrassment" in everyday matters of etiquette and manners, and the earlier diaries particularly, as she makes her entrance into the world, are full of them; but they often hint at a more deep-seated dread and are not always comic or always comically treated. At the age of sixteen she is "frighten'd to death" at being asked to open a Ball, but successfully escapes. She cannot describe her embarrassment on a visit to the theatre when she hears two lines in praise of *Cecilia* included in the epilogue. As she says on another occasion, she was "flattered but fluttered", and the closeness of the words nicely catches what for her was always the closeness of the things – being noticed and feeling shamed. She describes her great shyness at entering a room full of people and admits she is always embarrassed when attention is paid to her; and since she was always receiving attention as the authoress of *Evelina* and *Cecilia*, "embarrassing situations" (a phrase she often used) were frequent. Fanny Burney never out-grew her dread of being noticed. In a journal-letter of 1814 she notes that "never yet had the moment arrived in which to be marked had not been embarrassing and disconcerting to me, even when most flattering"; and a year later she can still say of a small incident that "In a situation of such embarrassment I never before was placed." She is "in an agony of fear and shame" at appearing in a few scenes in a play. She is embarrassed when before her marriage to d'Arblay she receives a letter from him in her father's unsuspicious presence, and frequently more embarrassed in her courtship with d'Arblay, "feeling my poor Cheeks as hot, and probably as red, as two burning Cinders". She remembers the shame and alarm when d'Arblay "entered from the Passage Door, and – my Mother hastily and pointedly retreated through her own". She is covered in shame when her three year old son behaves rumbustiously on a visit to the Queen, lies on the floor, capers round the room, hammers the furniture and disobeys the Royal command to leave his mother alone. Embarrassment becomes mortification when she is seen by the King and Queen talking to Boswell at Windsor and when she says or does anything that might cause her to lose the good opinion of others or even be brought to their notice. Mortification becomes shame when the attention paid to her is of too particular a kind, and it was part of a young woman's inevitable fate to receive this kind of attention. All her heroines receive it, but Fanny Burney's dramatization of a young woman's shame and fear is as vivid in the journals as in the fiction. A longer extract from *The Early Diary* to illustrate her skill in this and other ways will show how her diaries and journal-letters provide much of the "essential material" of the novelist and how in them she learns the art of fiction.[27]

In May 1775 she was introduced to a young man called Mr Barlow. He struck her as good-tempered and sensible; she was told that his disposition and morals were excellent but she remained unimpressed:

> He has read more than he has conversed, and seems to know but little of the world; his language therefore is stiff and uncommon, and seems laboured, if not affected – he has a great desire to please, but no elegance of manners; neither, though he may be very worthy, is he at all agreeable.
>
> (*ED*, ii, 47)

The next day life begins to imitate literature when Mr Barlow's desire to please takes the form of a declaration of love in a letter whose cluttered, pompous prose makes the style of Mr Collins in *Pride and Prejudice* seem limpid. (It is probably a mistake to look to literary sources for Mr Collins's fatuousness; the real thing was always to hand.) Fanny Burney is not remembering the letter but transcribing it in full. "Madame," he writes to her,

> Uninterrupted happiness we are told is of a short duration, and is quickly succeeded by Anxiety, which moral Axiom I really experienc'd on the Conclusion of May day at Mr Charles Burney's, as the singular Pleasure of your Company was so soon Eclips'd by the rapidity of ever-flying Time; but the felicity, tho' short, was too great to keep within the limits of one Breast . . .
>
> (ibid., ii, 49)

This, and much more, from Mr Barlow's "ardorous Pen". The complete letter helps to establish Mr Barlow's character in this novel-like scene with the young woman (Fanny Burney is twenty-five) having to defend herself against an unwanted and foolish suitor. As in *Evelina* and *Pride and Prejudice* the scene is a comic one, but the very real predicament of the heroine (the word is inevitable even when talking about the journals) makes a happy ending far from certain. Fanny Burney writes a letter of refusal but she must have her father's permission to send it. When he first reads Mr Barlow's flourishes he is "all indulgence to his daughter" and she therefore does not understand why he wants her to delay her answer. She knows that her father cannot think well of Mr Barlow, and it is only later that she learns with dismay that "he was unwilling I should give a No without some further knowledge of the young man". (Dr Burney was, like Mr Bennet, in the familiar position of having several daughters but very little to leave them, and unlike Mr Bennet he worried about their future. It was this worry which made him delight in Fanny Burney's court appointment and blind to the misery of her five long years.) Further knowledge, however, will in this case be of no avail: "the *heart* ought to be heard, and mine will never speak a word I am sure, for any one I do not truly enough honour to cheerfully, in all things serious, obey". She could, in a way, afford these fine sentiments, for although Mr Crisp distressed her by urging her to listen to Mr Barlow, and although she knew that everyone was "kindly interested in her welfare" – that is, hoped to see her marry him – she had in spite of a moment's anxiety one important consolation: "Everybody is against me but my beloved father." Dr Burney would not interfere further, but the pressure of society mounts. Mr Crisp now enters the drama as a worldly-wise tempter. Mr Barlow is a good catch. "You may live to the age of your grandmother, and not meet with so valuable an offer." Fanny should look around her; or better still, "look at your aunts", or the even more unfortunate Mrs Hamilton who "once had an offer of £3000 a-year, or near it; a parcel of young giggling girls laugh'd her out of it". Mr Crisp is earnest, even sombre: "Suppose you to lose your father, – take in all chances. Consider the situation of an unprotected, unprovided woman!" The chance is a great one; "For God's sake, give yourself fair play." (Charlotte Lucas did all this, took Mr Collins and "felt all the good luck of it".)

With the situation now explained and the characters established the comic but tense drama of embarrassment begins. To avoid a social call the following day where she might meet Mr Barlow Fanny Burney invents a cold (without telling her mother) and stays at home; but this only postpones a scene with the persistent suitor, for a visitor is announced the next day:

> I guessed who it was – and was inexpressibly confused. Mama stared but desired he might walk in. The door opened, and Mr Barlow appeared. He had dressed himself elegantly, but could hardly speak. He bowed two or three times – I coloured like

scarlet, and I believe he was the only person in the room who did
not see it.

"Mrs. O'Connor – he called – my cold – he understood – he was
very sorry" –

He could not get on. My voice failed me terribly – for his silence
at his first entrance made me fear he was going to reproach me for
not answering his letter. I told him my cold had been too bad to
allow me to go out – but I was so terribly frightened lest my
mother should say – *"What cold? I did not know you had one!"* – that I
had great difficulty to get out the words; and he himself took
notice that my *voice* spoke how bad my cold was, though in fact I
have no cold at all, but grew *husky* from embarrassment. My
mother then asked him to sit down and Sukey, very good
naturedly entered into conversation with him to our mutual relief
– particularly to his, as he seemed so confounded he scarce knew
where he was. I sat upon thorns from the fear that he would desire
to speak to me alone. I looked another way, and hardly opened
my mouth. In about half an hour he rose to go. . . . Whether he
was induced to make this visit from expecting he might speak to
me, or whether in order to see if I had any cold or not, I cannot tell;
but it proved cruelly distressing to him, and confusing to me.

Had I sent an answer, this would not have happened; but it is
now too late.

(ED, ɪɪ, 55–6)

A brief second meeting with Mr Barlow passes without mention of
his unanswered letter but with a hint that he knows her cold was a
tactical one. (Fanny Burney is "not sorry that he thought *my cold* in
my own power".) About a week later he sends a second "high-
flown" letter. This now seems a good chance to end the whole
business, but before she writes she thinks it her duty to speak to her
father, "never doubting his immediate concurrence".

My mother, Sukey, and I went to the Opera that evening; it was
therefore too late when I returned to send a letter to Hoxton – but I
went up stairs into the study, and told my father I had received
another epistle from Mr. Barlow, which I could only attribute to
my not answering, as I had wished, his first. I added that I
proposed, with his leave, to write to Mr. Barlow the next
morning.

My father looked grave, asked me for the letter, put it in his pocket unread, and wished me good night.

I was seized with a kind of *pannic*. I trembled at the idea of his espousing, however mildly, the cause of this young man. I passed a restless night, and in the morning dared not write without his permission, which I was now half afraid to ask.

(*ED*, II, 63)

The next day at 2 o'clock the importunate Mr Barlow calls again. It is his third visit, the grand climax of the episode, and Fanny Burney now re-creates it in a manner indistinguishable from her fiction. Memory, imaginative selection and emphasis, interpretation of Mr Barlow's words and looks, vivid revelation of the flux and reflux of her own feelings now make that vivid dramatization of a young woman's embarrassments and fears which years later will be the cause of *Evelina*'s success.

I think I was never more distressed in my life – to have taken pains to avoid a private conversation so highly disagreeable to me, and at last to be forced into it at so unfavourable a juncture, for I had now *two* letters from him, both unanswered, and consequently open to his conjectures. I exclaimed – "Lord! how provoking! what shall I do?"

My father looked uneasy and perplexed: he said something about not being hasty, which I did not desire him to explain. Terrified lest he should hint at the advantage of an early establishment – like Mr. Crisp – quick from the study – but slow enough afterwards – I went down stairs. I saw my mother pass from the front into the back parlour; which did not add to the *graciousness* of my reception of poor Mr. Barlow, who I found alone in the front parlour. I was not sorry that none of the family were there, as I now began to seriously dread any protraction of this affair.

He came up to me with an air of *tenderness* and satisfaction, began some anxious enquiries about my health; but I interrupted him with saying – "I fancy, Sir, you have not received a letter I – I –"

I stopt, for I could not say which I had *sent*!

"A letter? – No, Ma'am!"

"You will have it, then, to-morrow, Sir."

We were both silent for a minute or two, when he said – "In consequence I presume, Ma'am, of the one I –"

"Yes, Sir," cried I.

"And pray – Ma'am – Miss Burney! – may I – beg to ask the contents? – that is – the – the –." He could not go on.

"Sir – I – it was only – it was merely – in short, you will see it to-morrow."

"But if you would favour me with the contents now, I could perhaps answer it at once?"

"Sir, it requires no answer!"

A second silence ensued. I was really distressed myself to see *his* distress, which was very apparent. After some time he stammered out something of *hoping*, and *beseeching* – which, gathering more firmness, I answered – 'I am much obliged to you, Sir, for the too good opinion you are pleased to have of me – but I should be very sorry you should lose any more time upon my account – as I have no thoughts of changing my situation and abode."

He seemed to be quite overset: having, therefore, so freely explained myself, I then asked him to sit down, and began to talk of the weather. When he had a little recovered himself, he drew a chair close to me and began making most ardent professions of respect and regard, and so forth. I interrupted him as soon as I could, and begged him to rest satisfied with my answer.

"*Satisfied?*" repeated he, "my dear Ma'am – is that possible?"

"Perhaps, Sir," said I, "I ought to make some apologies for not answering your first letter – but really I was so much surprised – upon so short an acquaintance."

He then began making excuses for having written; but as to *short acquaintance*, he owned it was a reason for *me* – but for *him* – fifty years could not have more convinced him of my, &c. &c.

"You have taken a sudden, and far too partial idea of my character," answered I. "If you look round among your older acquaintance, I doubt not but you will very soon be able to make a better choice."

He shook his head: "I have seen Madam, a great many ladies, it is true – but never –"

"You do me much honour," cried I, "but I must desire you would take no further trouble about me – for I have not at present the slightest thoughts of ever leaving this house."

"*At present?*" repeated he, eagerly. "No, I would not expect it – I would not wish to precipitate – but in future –"

"Neither now or ever, Sir," returned I, "have I any view of changing my condition."

"But surely, surely this can never be! so severe a resolution – you cannot mean it – it would be wronging all the world!"

"I am extremely sorry, Sir, that you did not receive my letter, because it might have saved you this trouble."

He looked very much mortified, and said in a dejected voice – "If there is anything in me – in my connexions – or in my situation in life, which you wholly think unworthy of you – and beneath you – or if my character, or disposition meet with your disapprobation – I will immediately forgo all – I will not – I would not –"

"No, indeed, Sir," cried I, "I have neither seen or heard of anything of you that was to your disadvantage – and I have no doubts of your worthiness –"

He thanked me, and seemed reassured; but renewed his solicitations in the most urgent manner. He repeatedly begged my permission to acquaint my family of the state of his affairs, and to abide by their decision; but I would not let him say two words following upon that subject. I told him that my answer was a final one, and begged him to take it as such.

He remonstrated very earnestly. "This is the severest decision! . . . Surely you must allow that the *social state* is what we were all meant for? – that we were created for one another? that to form such a resolution is contrary to the design of our being?" –

"All this may be true," said I, "I have nothing to say in contradiction to it – but you know there are many odd characters in the world – and I am one of them."

'O, no, no, no, – that can never be! but is it possible that you can have so bad an opinion of the Married State? It seems to me the *only* state for happiness!"

"Well, Sir *you* are attracted to the married life – I am to the single – therefore *every man in his humour* – do you follow *your* opinion – and let *me* follow *mine*."

"But, surely – is not this *singular?*"

"I give you leave, Sir," cried I, laughing, "to think me singular – odd – queer – nay, even whimsical, if you please."

"But, my dear Miss Burney, only –"

"I entreat you, Sir, to take my answer – you really pain me by being so urgent."

"That would not I do for the world! – I only beg you to suffer me – perhaps in future –"

"No, indeed, I shall never change – I do assure you you will find me very obstinate!"

He began to lament his own destiny. I grew extremely tired of so often saying the same thing; but I could not absolutely turn him out of the house; and, indeed, he seemed so dejected and unhappy, that I made it my study to soften my refusal as much as I could without leaving room for future expectations.

About this time my mother came in. We both rose. I was horridly provoked at my situation.

"I am only come in for a letter," cried she, "pray don't let me disturb you." And away she went . . .

This could not but be encouraging to him, for she was no sooner gone than he began again the same story, and seemed determined not to give up his cause. He hoped, at least, that I would allow him to enquire after my health?

"I must beg you, Sir, to send me no more letters."

He seemed much hurt, and looked down in silence.

"You had better, Sir, think of me no more, if you study your own happiness –"

"I *do* study my own happiness – more than I have ever had any probability of doing before!"

"You have made an unfortunate choice, Sir, but you will find it easier to forget it than you imagine. You have only to suppose that I was not at Mr. Burney's on May Day – and it was a mere chance my being there – and then you will be –"

"But, if I *could*, – could I also forget seeing you at old Mrs. Burney's? – and if I did – can I forget that I see you now?"

"O yes! In three months' time you may forget you ever saw me. You will not find it so difficult as you suppose."

"You have heard, Ma'am, of an old man being ground young? Perhaps you believe *that*? But you will not deny me leave to sometimes see you?"

"My father, Sir, is seldom, hardly ever, indeed, at home."

"I have never seen the Doctor – but I hope he would not refuse me the permission to enquire after your health? I have no wish without his consent."

"Though I acknowledge myself to be *singular* I would not have you think me either affected or *trifling*, – and therefore I must assure you I am *fixed* in the answer I have given you – *unalterably* fixed."

His entreaties grew more extremely . . . distressing to me. He besought me to take more time, and said it should be the study of his life to make me happy. "Allow me, my *dear* Miss Burney, only to hope that my future conduct –"

"I shall always think myself obliged, nay, honoured by your good opinion – and you are entitled to my best wishes for your health and happiness – but, indeed, the less we meet the better."

"What – what can I do?" cried he very sorrowfully.

"Why – go and *ponder* upon this affair for about half an hour. Then say – what an odd, queer, strange creature she is – and then – think of something else."

'O no, no! – you cannot suppose all that? I shall think of nothing else; – your refusal is more pleasing than any other lady's acceptance –"

He said this very simply, but too seriously for me to laugh at. Just then, Susette came in – but did not stay two minutes. It would have been shocking to be thus left purposely as if with a declared lover, and then I was not sorry to have an opportunity of preventing future doubts and expectations . . .

He then took his leave: – returned back; – took leave; – and returned again. I now made a more formal reverence of the head, at the same time expressing my good wishes for his welfare, in a sort of way that implied I expected never to see him again. He would fain have taken a more *tender* leave of me, – but I repulsed him with great surprise and displeasure. I did not, however, as he was so terribly sorrowful refuse him my hand, which he had made sundry attempts to take in the course of conversation. When I withdrew it, as I did presently, I rang the bell to prevent his again returning from the door.

Though I was really sorry for the unfortunate and misplaced attachment which this young man professes for me, yet I could almost have *jumped* for joy when he was gone, to think that the affair was thus finally over.

(*ED*, II, 64–8)

Not quite over, however. She has not yet had a chance to speak to her father; and when she does, he surprises her, and comedy gives way briefly to dread.

The next day, a day, the remembrance of which will be never erased from my memory, – my father first spoke to me *in favour* of Mr. Barlow, and desired me not to be *peremptory* in the answer I was going to write, though it was to appear written previously.

I scarce made any answer; I was terrified to death. I felt the utter impossibility of resisting not merely my father's *persuasion*, but even his *advice*. I felt too, that I had no argumentative objections to make to Mr. Barlow, his character – disposition – situation – I know nothing against; but, O! I felt he was no companion for my heart! I wept like an infant, when alone; eat nothing; seemed as if already married, and passed the whole day in more misery than, merely on my own account, I ever did before in my life, except when a child, upon the loss of my own beloved mother, and ever revered and most dear grandmother!

(ED, ii, 69)

Then the final development when she goes after supper to wish her father good-night, "which I did as cheerfully as I could, though pretty evidently in dreadful uneasiness".

When I had got to the door, he called me back, and asked some questions concerning a new Court mourning gown . . . kindly saying he would assist Susey and me in our fitting-out, which he accordingly did, and affectionately embraced me, saying, "I wish I could do more for thee, Fanny!" "Oh, Sir;" cried I, "*I* wish for nothing! only let me live with you." "My life!" cried he, kissing me kindly, "Thou shalt live with me for ever, if thee wilt! Thou canst not think I meant to get rid of thee?"

"I could not Sir; I could not!" cried I; "I could not outlive such a thought!" and, as I kissed him – O! how gratefully and thankfully! with what a relief to my heart! I saw his eyes full of tears! a mark of his tenderness which I shall never forget! "God knows," continued he, "I wish not to part with my girls! only, don't be too hasty!"

Thus relieved, restored to future hopes, I went to bed, light, happy, and thankful, as if escaped from destruction.

(ED, ii, 70)

Fanny Burney had already written (but not sent) a short letter of refusal to Mr Barlow before speaking to her father. The letter is now despatched and her distress is over: "From that day to this my father, I thank Heaven, has never again mentioned Mr. Barlow."

We read these pages from her diary as we read a novel. We can admire the clearly etched characters and enjoy the pages of dialogue imaginatively reconstructed (as we know) from a few brief notes and yet always convincing. It is the faint oddity of Mr Barlow's remark, "*your* refusal is more pleasing than any other lady's acceptance", which persuades us of its accuracy. We can admire the unobtrusive art of selection and emphasis which sustains the drama and avoids tedium. Mr Barlow was a very wordy man, but we notice that his "ardent professions of respect and regard" are merely acknowledged and not retailed to the reader; that Fanny Burney frequently interrupts what threatens to be a tiresome speech (was it really as easy as this to cut him short?), and that when she has given a slight flavour of his verbosity she spares us the rest with "etc. etc." in order that the snip-snap of dialogue may be resumed and that we may not lose, any more than she does, all sympathy with Mr Barlow. He must not be allowed to bore us as Colonel Goldsworthy does or we could not understand Fanny Burney when she notes that "I was really distressed myself to see *his* distress". We can admire, too, the way in which the separate episodes in the story of Mr Barlow's abortive courtship are shaped to a climax of anxiety and then to a final happy issue from all her afflictions. We read these pages as we read a novel and forget that the anxieties controlled here by art were, indeed, her personal afflictions – and of a common kind. Mr Barlow's insistence plagues and distresses her. She is "terrified to death" when her father advises her not to be peremptory in the letter she will write, because she knows the impossibility of going against such advice. "A kind of pannic" and a misery, greater than any she has known since the death of her mother, make the whole day one which will never be erased from her memory. The build-up of her unhappiness makes her father's relenting a sudden shock of delight; but still the final word is of her escape from "destruction".

This powerful word is the accurate word. The essential material of the novels which is everywhere found in the journals is not the small (or even large) everyday confusions and embarrassments or the worries about behaviour and manners, but the imagination of a larger disaster, the dread of an always threatening destruction of the self which could come (as in the Mr Barlow episode) from a loveless marriage (she knows nothing against him, "but, O! I felt he was no companion of my heart") from losing through disobedience or rebellion the love of those on whom she depended, and from the intolerable strain (after five years at court she could not tolerate it) of being at all times and in all places "expected to display modesty, reserve, submission, and at the same time to possess the active qualities plainly needed for survival".[28] The essential material of journals and novels, what Patricia Meyer Spacks calls their "underlying principle of coherence",[29] is the position of a young woman making her entrance into the world where with limited, limiting choices she must submit but assert herself, "blot out personality" yet avoid destruction. In a diary entry in 1769 she writes: "How truly does this Journal contain my real and undisguised thoughts!";[30] but, in fact, through indirection the novels tell us more about her own position and dilemmas and those of other women. It is true in Fanny Burney's case that "more emphatically than fiction, eighteenth-century autobiographies reveal the claims women wish to make".[31] Her diaries and journals and letters are, indeed, a lengthy autobiography; but it is the novels which allow her "to enlarge the communication of her own nature"[32] and which best reveal the restrictions imposed upon women and Fanny Burney's regulated anger at women's limited choices and society's repressive expectations. The anonymity of her novels (*Evelina* had no attribution: the later novels were simply "by the author of *Evelina*") gave a protection which journals and letters could not provide. It is true that the authorship of *Evelina* soon became an open secret and that the authorship of the later novels was never a secret at all, but the self-concealment of fiction made possible a safer, subtler self-revelation and protest.

Safer in a very obvious way. The letters were, of course, meant to be read, but the private diaries, even the diary addressed to Nobody, might be discovered and the "real and undisguised thoughts" revealed. And this is what happened. By mistake Fanny Burney left an early page of her most private diary, the diary to Nobody, on the piano where it was found by her father who read it and teased her before returning it. She herself was not greatly upset; she says she was "in a sad distress", but her account of the affair is sprightly and entertainingly comic. A few days later a family friend, Miss Young, advised Fanny Burney to give up journal-writing as it was "the most dangerous employment young persons can have . . .

it makes them often record things which ought *not* to be recorded, but instantly forgot". Fanny Burney's defence is that her father "knows that I *do* write and what I write". She then offers to let Miss Young read any part of the journal; and though she makes the suggestion "with shame and fear" it is only because she thinks her journal "nonsense" and not worth reading. Miss Young reads it, approves of it and finds it "harmless".[33] Her father's unconcern, Miss Young's verdict and Fanny Burney's chatty good-humour make us wonder how "real and undisguised" her thoughts really were, or perhaps show us that in these early diaries she had no resentments to discover, no anger to regulate. She was, after all, at this time just sixteen. She had little to complain about and there are few critical or even dry comments on people, society or the demands made upon young women. A hint of irritation at the endless social visits to boring people – "Miss Hurrell is an obliging, civil, tiresome woman" – reminds us once every two hundred pages of Jane Austen's letters.

There is, indeed, a lengthier protest, an attack on custom in her first diary in 1769:

> Miss Crawford called here lately – she is very earnest for us to visit her – but *we* are not very earnest about the matter: – however, the code of custom make our spending one evening with her necessary. O! how I hate this vile custom which obliges us to make slaves of ourselves! – to sell the most precious property we boast, our time; – and to sacrifice it to every prattling impertinent who chooses to demand it! – Yet those who shall pretend to defy this irksome confinement of our happiness, must stand accused of incivility, – breach of manners – love of originality, – and . . . what not. . . . For why should we not be permitted to be masters of our time? – Why may we not venture to love, and to dislike – and why, if we do, may we not give to those we love the richest jewel we own, our time?
>
> (*ED*, I, 54)

Spacks quotes this passage as a contribution by Fanny Burney (at the age of seventeen) to the "condition of women" question, but omits the first sentence which makes clear that Fanny Burney's is a local irritation at being obliged to make a return social call on someone she dislikes (Jane Austen's letters are full of such complaints), and omits a sentence at the end of the passage which shows how slight and trivial Fanny Burney knew the irritation to be: custom "in short, is a very ridiculous affair, more particularly as it hath kept me writing on it till I have forgot what introduced it". But even such local irritation or vexation is rare in the diaries and journals, early or late. The diaries, after all, were pronounced "harmless". Very much more common is the kind of reaction she had four years later to Miss Bowdler who is considered sensible, clever and witty, but who "reckons herself superior to the opinion of the world and to all common forms and customs". Fanny Burney agrees with the opinion that anyone who despises the customs and manners of the country she lives in "must, consequently, conduct herself with impropriety". It is nice that the great Dr Bowdler's sister should be able to shock Fanny Burney who finds her behaviour "highly improper"; and though it is agreed that her conduct is totally innocent when she visits the house of friends who have a young man as a lodger, Fanny Burney "can by no means approve so great a contempt of public opinion".

Anger and criticism are rare in the diaries, and even when they occur rebellion goes no further than their expression. In 1780 she expresses something close to contempt for the fashionable set at Bath: "My coldness in return to all these sickening, heartless, *ton*-led people, I try not to repress, though to treat them with such respect as their superior stations fairly claim, I would not for the world neglect."[34] The admission of showing coldness to people (who since they are heartless would not notice it) is confined to the privacy of the diary. This problem of balancing the demands of society and the needs of the individual is a common one in women's fiction of the time, though often no balance is won. (Sometimes the imbalance is the heroine's self-immolation on the altar of a quixotic honour.) Elinor in chapter seventeen of *Sense and Sensibility* manages this balance and is scorned by Marianne for her pains:

> "But I thought it was right, Elinor," said Marianne, "to be guided wholly by the opinion of other people. I thought our judgments were given us merely to be subservient to those of our neighbours. This has always been your doctrine, I am sure."
> "No, Marianne, never. My doctrine has never aimed at the subjection of the understanding. All I have ever attempted to influence has been the behaviour. You must not confound my meaning. I am guilty, I confess, of having often wished you to treat our acquaintance in general with greater attention; but when

have I advised you to adopt their sentiments or conform to their judgment in serious matters?"

Fanny Burney goes further than Elinor; what she aims at in the diaries is often "the subjection of the understanding", conformity in thought word and deed. Unlike Elinor she was possessed and governed by fear. She knew it herself: "A fear of doing wrong has always been the leading principle of my internal guidance", and the same fear teaches how to avoid all risk of it. In 1788 "Mr Turbulent" (a nickname for a friend) says that she has been saved from all wrong-doing by prejudice, education and accident; but again she knows better: "Perhaps so", cried I. "And one thing more, I acknowledge myself obliged to, on various occasions – Fear. I run no risks that I see – I run – but it is always away from all danger that I perceive."[35] Fear of doing wrong is matched by fear of even thinking wrong; she seldom permits herself a thought that might be "singular", and when she does she at once distances herself from it. Miss Young did not need to worry about Fanny Burney's diaries; in them nothing is recorded which ought not be recorded. Her usual practice is to write about the self but run away from it and avoid self-revelation; she is at once loquacious and reticent. Too often her judgments are, for safety's sake, close to those of her neighbours. Too often her fears lead her close to the subjection of her understanding; but in the novels Fanny Burney's understanding found ways of avenging itself.

The letters and journals which Fanny Burney wrote at court show how little her autobiographical writings "reveal the claims women wish to make", how little they contain her "real and undisguised thoughts", how much more difficult than in the novels it was to make any protest or achieve any balance between the demands of others and the needs of the self. In these years, indeed, the self was nearly destroyed and a complete nervous breakdown narrowly avoided. The greater reason she had to complain, the greater her silence; the greater cause she had for weeping, the more determined she was to die rather than weep. Nearly her only defence, as these journals show, was surrender. The royal invitation to become Second Keeper of the Robes was one that could not be refused. Her father saw that this first royal favour to his daughter might, if accepted, be followed by offers and favours to his other children who all still had their way to make in the world. Fanny Burney could not refuse it and could not "even to my father utter my reluctance, –

I see him so much delighted . . .''. She could see the worldly advantages of the post but it was not these that persuaded her:

> To have declined such a proposal would . . . have been thought madness and folly, – nor, indeed, should I have been *permitted* to decline it, without exciting a displeasure that must have made me quite unhappy.[36]

Here was a danger from which she could not run away. Escape had always been her way of assertion and at court this would not be possible. To restore herself by describing her new servitude in letters and journals became more and more difficult. To disobey or disoblige her father was always impossible; to disoblige the King and Queen or give a hint of ingratitude or complaint was unthinkable. In these years she wrote a lengthy court diary which contains much of her most entertaining writing. In it are the lengthy accounts of the Warren Hastings trial and the dramatically vivid scenes of the King's illness; and there is the same skill in creating character and conversation through her superb gifts of memory and selection. Even when she is ill she sets out to show "in genuine colours, a Royal sailor" (the Duke of Clarence) and to give "an idea of the energy of his Royal Highness's language". The energy is beautifully caught; and one sign of it must particularly have pleased her when the Duke interrupted Mrs Schwellenberg with the words, "Hold you your potato-jaw, my Dear".[37] But at the heart of the journal is a silence about herself; and for many months, when because of depression and illness scarcely even a memorandum was made, the silence was literal and almost complete. When she most needed to survive, her customary life-saver – the act of writing – failed her. In these years especially she seldom allowed herself to assert her "real and undisguised thoughts". Her defence was not protest but repression, and there was much to repress.

Her mood and intention, her way of defence and the reason for her silence are clear in a diary entry for the first day of 1787 when she had already spent six miserable months at court:

> MONDAY, JANUARY 1st. – I opened the new year with what composure I could acquire. I considered it as the first year of my being settled in a permanent situation, and made anew the best resolutions I was equal to forming, that I would do what I could

to curb all spirit of repining, and to content myself calmly – unresistingly, at least – with my destiny.

(*Diary*, III, 229)

An unpublished letter to her sister Esther in December 1786 (quoted by Joyce Hemlow) shows how soon at court she felt despair and misery, much of which was caused by her superior, Mrs Schwellenberg. Fanny Burney had not realized that when she was not attending the Queen she was expected to be the autocratic Mrs Schwellenberg's "companion, her Humble Companion, at her own command!". But she cannot risk either her father's disappointment or the Queen's disapproval, and so she continues: "You see, then, my situation; *Here I must remain!* The die is cast, – and That struggle is no more . . .". Neither her father nor the Queen is blamed, though others were quick to blame them. Neither knew of Mrs Schwellenberg's cruelty and neither could be told:

Little does the Queen know the Slavery I must either resist or bear. And so frightful is Hostility. . . . Can you read me? I blot and re-write – yet know not how to alter or what to send.[38]

Fanny Burney suffered more than any of her heroines. To the everyday mental suffering she caused, Mrs Schwellenberg added physical suffering. On a coach journey from Windsor to London in the winter of 1787 she insisted on leaving open the window on Fanny Burney's side of the coach, "whence there blew in a sharp wind, which so painfully attacked my eyes that they were inflamed even before we arrived in town". Fanny Burney does not protest ("it was among the evils that I can always best bear") because the only way of escape – resignation from her post – was impossible, and so another kind of resignation is her only resource. She had the consolation of describing in her journal Mrs Schwellenberg's "ill-humour, violence and rudeness",[39] but such relief was impossible with the Queen's much more dangerous, unconscious cruelty.

By 1790 Fanny Burney's illness was something much worse than inflammation of the eyes; in a rare meeting with her father (life at court was a polite imprisonment with very few visitors allowed) she confessed that she was suffering from physical exhaustion ("I was worn with want of rest, and fatigued with laborious watchfulness and attendance") from loneliness ("was dead to all domestic

endearment") and from deep misery ("happiness was excluded").
Her father at once allowed her to resign her post, but fifteen more
months of servitude and worsening health passed before she could
bring herself to present her letter of resignation, or "memorial" to
the Queen and before a successor could be found. The physical
symptoms of her sickness were debilitation and fatigue: "langour,
feverish nights, and restless days were incessant"; but still she
waited to present her "memorial". She would rather lose her health
than the Queen's favour. By December she had frequent pains in
her side and difficulty in breathing. Her depression of spirits and
her "extreme alteration of person" should have made it easy for her;
"for I saw no one, except my Royal Mistress and Mrs Schwellenberg
who noticed not the change . . . but as they alone saw it not, or
mentioned it not, that afforded me no resource", and her loss of
health "was now so notorious, that no part of the house could
wholly avoid acknowledging it". Not even the Queen? Fanny
Burney takes every care not to blame the Queen for blindness; or
perhaps takes no care at all, but simply does not see or will not see
anything to blame in her conduct. Even when the Queen must have
known ("Her Majesty was very kind during this time") she did not
think of releasing her unhappy captive: "for though I was frequently
so ill in her presence that I could hardly stand, I saw she concluded
me, while life remained, inevitably hers".[40] Meanwhile her friends
were shocked at her obvious ill-health and pressed her to quit her
position. Wyndham spoke to her father and suggested to her
brother that elopement would be the quickest way to manage her
escape. Horace Walpole urged her to leave her "closet at Court",
where, he said shrewdly, "you will still discover mankind, though
not disclose it"; and Boswell tried to bustle her into leaving: "My
dear ma'am, why do you stay? – it won't do ma'am! you must resign!
– we can put up with it no longer."[41] Even when her "memorial"
was accepted, Fanny Burney's continued attendance was
vigorously required to the very day of her departure. In June 1791
the Queen was still insisting on a further fortnight's duty from her
though Fanny Burney now stood with such "infinite difficulty in the
Queen's presence . . . that I was obliged to be dismissed". In a diary
entry for her last week of court bondage in July 1791, but written
after her return to her father's house, the strain of her refusal to
confess her "real and undisguised thoughts" – perhaps her inability
to know them – and her dread of incurring disapproval, dislike or
displeasure reach a tired climax:

JULY. – I come now to write the last week of my Royal residence. The Queen honoured me with the most uniform graciousness, and though, as the time of separation approached, her cordiality rather diminished, and traces of internal displeasure appeared sometimes, arising from an opinion I ought rather to have struggled on, live or die, than to quit her, – yet I am sure she saw how poor was my own chance, except by a change in the mode of life, and at least ceased to wonder, though she could not approve.

(*Diary*, v, 178)

The editor of the *Diary* says that Fanny Burney employed "the best means with which she was acquainted, for bringing her feelings into accordance with her judgment", and, certainly, even in her journals for the court years she could not be happy unless they coincided; but as a result her feelings were often suppressed, her judgment strained and her "real and undisguised" thoughts difficult to find. She had said earlier that she would try to content herself "unresistingly" with her destiny, and in fact she offered little resistance; she could not run away and she did not recover herself in writing. There were long silences in her journals and she made only the briefest preliminary notes for *Camilla*. Instead of fiction she now wrote several blank-verse tragedies which may, as Joyce Hemlow says, have provided "emotional outlets for the dreary years", but which are an escape from the world and from herself, and not, like the novels and some of her other autobiographical writings, imaginatively accurate reconstructions of the position of woman in society. Fanny Burney found the writing of them "a solace, a blessing" because they "beguiled me of myself". Diffidence and daring are the marks of her novels, but in the journals at this time there is only diffidence. "Self-discovery of a woman in hiding"[42] may be the subject of the novels as of the journals, but in these pages there is only a deeper hiding.

The years at court were, it is true, very special years ("my mind was a stranger to rest") and there were special reasons for her caution; but though scarcely any other woman in England experienced the killingly restrictive conditions of court life, these years focus with particular sharpness the essential condition of a woman in English society who, like Miss Bates in *Emma*, was "neither young, handsome, rich nor married". They focus sharply, too, the limitations of all her journals, of the journal form itself as she practised it. In the autobiographical writings (and most obviously in the court journals) direct criticism of a woman's lot was almost impossible; indeed it seems that the harsher her lot, the more difficult Fanny Burney found direct protest of any kind. The very act of writing was seen by her as rebellion enough. A very rare silent scream betrays the unbearable, boring servitude of her mindless routine as Assistant Keeper of the Robes, but even this breaks from her only when she is ill: "And – O picquet! – life hardly hangs on earth during its compulsion, in these months succeeding months, and years creeping, crawling, after years."[43] Just as rarely can she distance herself from her own unhappiness, see herself (as she did in her first interview with the King) as "acting in play" and so write comically (and therefore critically) about the restraints imposed upon her. It is true that in a sprightly letter to her sister she gives instructions on how one is expected to comport oneself in the royal presence, and in particular she gives

Directions for coughing, sneezing, or moving, before the King and Queen.
  In the first place, you must not cough. If you find a cough tickling in your throat, you must arrest it from making any sound; if you find yourself choking with the forbearance, you must choke – but not cough.
  In the second place, you must not sneeze. If you have a vehement cold, you must take no notice of it; if your nose-membranes feel a great irritation, you must hold your breath; if a sneeze still insists upon making its way, you must oppose it, by keeping your teeth grinding together; if the violence of the repulse breaks some blood-vessel, you must break the blood-vessel – but not sneeze.

(*Diary*, ii, 345–6)

This is dry, detached and critical, but it was written some months before she took up her appointment and some weeks before she suspected that such an appointment was possible. This kind of control or self-suppression contained no threat; she could always avoid the need for it by avoiding the occasion. She was not, after all, obliged to meet the King and Queen; if she wished (and she generally did wish) she could always run away from the danger:

In the midst of all this the Queen came!

I heard the thunder at the door, and, panic struck, away flew all
my resolutions and agreements, and away after them flew I!

(*Diary*, II, 312)

And even when some hours later a second "intended retreat" was
cut off by the King, she "diverted" herself with "a thousand
ridiculous notions, of my own situation". Once at court, however,
escape and dryness (another form of escape) were impossible, and
she had no other resource, no indirect means (as she found in the
novels) by which the heart in hiding could proclaim itself.

In a surprising diary entry in 1805 Fanny Burney notes that
although her son had enjoyed a certain comedy by the French
dramatist, Poisson, he was too young "to enter into the sport of
disguised satire and ambiguous irony".[44] It is surprising because
she was not an ironic writer, yet irony could have helped her to
remain hidden but assertive and could have been the indirection by
which she might find direction out. Irony is almost as absent from
her journals and novels as satire. Where satire occurs in her journals
or fiction it is always on the fringes and never at the heart of the
writing. Captain Mirvan and Madame Duval are satirically sketched
in *Evelina*, but their power to hurt the heroine is small; they
embarrass but do not threaten her. There is no satire, however, of
those like Sir Clement Willoughby whose sexual harassment is the
continuous unavoidable threat to the heroine's survival and to the
book's comedy. In a diary entry for 1773 Fanny Burney says of a
clerical acquaintance that "his love of ease is surpassed by nothing,
but his love of good living, which equals whatever detraction has
hitherto devised for a parson's gluttony"; but there is no satire in the
same diary of the attitudes and behaviour expected of a young
woman making her entrance into the world. The *Directions for
coughing* is, indeed, satire; but such directions caused only physical
discomfort and were not exclusively intended for women. Satire is a
form of aggression and Fanny Burney's instinct and method led her
to hide, to "run no risks that I perceive". Satire was also unfeeling.
She says of a friend in 1815 that she had "a turn to satire that made
the defects of her neighbours rather afford her amusement than
concern" (like Jane Austen in her letters) and Fanny Burney
preferred in fiction "the exquisite refinement of quick sensibility".
Irony was more dangerous still. She calls it "ambiguous"; it is
therefore subversive and she did not wish to subvert. "While I stand
fast in points of honour, I must content myself to relinquish those of

inclination."[45] Irony, being ambiguous, might bring the risk of being misunderstood, of being thought to endorse the very things she feared and of which she disapproved. In her autobiographical writings her only way of facing what shocked or displeased her was by turning away from it; the intact, unambiguous preservation of her moral simplicity, her monochrome morality, made any indirect or comic handling of such things impossible.

Fanny Burney loved the theatre but was often shocked by the plays she saw. Farquhar's *Sir Harry Wildair* is "a very disagreeable play, and wholly abounding in all that can do violence to innocence and morality". Far too frequently "I meet with too much disgust in all Fielding's dramatic works to . . . laugh at his wit", and, in any case, "I should never myself think it worth wading through so much dirt to get at." Walpole's *The Mysterious Mother* gets her "heaviest censure" and so shocks her that she wants to run away not only from the play, but from the author as well whom she now almost regards "as the patron of the vices he had been pleased to record".[46] It was the fear of wrong-doing and of wrong-thinking which, she said, had saved her from doing and thinking wrong ("I run no risks that I see – I run"), and the very title of a play or novel could rush her into retreat. In 1783, when she was thirty-one, a Mr J— asked her if she had read "the new book that has had such a run in France, 'Les Liaisons dangéreuses [sic]'?" and which had been published in France the previous year. In a rapid but aggressively defensive retreat Fanny Burney disposes of the novel, its author and poor Mr J—:

"No," answered I, not much pleased at the name, "I have not even heard of it."

"Indeed! – it has made so much noise in France I am quite surprised at that. It is not, indeed, a work that recommends very strict morality: but you, we all know, may look into any work without being hurt by it."

I felt hurt then, however, and very gravely answered, –

"I cannot give myself that praise, as I never look into any books that could hurt me . . ."

"This book was written by an officer; and he says, there are no characters or situations in it that he has not himself seen."

"That, then," cried I, "will with me always be a reason to as little desire seeing the officer as his book" . . . I only spoke to him in answer, after this little dialogue.   (*Diary*, II, 193)

It was not only from people and scenes in literature that she turned away in shocked disapproval; life could present equally dreadful dangers. There was always, for example the risk of meeting an adulteress. She had had to avoid Mme de Staël, whom she liked, when her *liaison dangereuse* with the Comte de Narbonne became known; and there was an awkward moment in the summer of 1791 when two English adulteresses, Lady Duncannon and Lady Forster appeared at a party given by Fanny Burney's friend Lady Spencer. Lady Duncannon's arrival "was the last thing that I could have wished" and Fanny Burney records her "unconquerable repugnance" at being in the same room. When Lady Duncannon moved to a nearer chair Fanny Burney announced that she herself "preferred moving about" and promptly moved about to see the children in the garden. Lady Forster is worse: only capital letters can do her justice (or perhaps injustice) for "INFAMY enwraps" her and her lover (the Duke of Devonshire). Fanny Burney first runs away morally – "I am satisfied her general powers of shining were violently damped by my coldness" – and then physically, to another corner of the room.[47] The contrast with Jane Austen's meeting an adulteress at a ball in Bath in 1801 is irresistible:

> I then got Mr Evelyn to talk to, and Miss Twistleton to look at; and I am proud to say that I have a very good eye for an Adultress, for tho' repeatedly assured that another in the same party was the *She*, I fixed upon the right one from the first. . . . She is not so pretty as I expected; her face has the same defect of baldness as her sister's, and her features not so handsome; – she was highly rouged, and looked rather quietly and contentedly silly than anything else.[48]

Fanny Burney had no aegis of irony to protect her and allow her the concealed expression of "the possible other case" for women or the "real and undisguised thoughts" of a young woman making her entrance into the world. In her diary for 1786 she admits that, after quarrelling with her, Mrs Schwellenberg misrepresented her to the Queen; but she "determined to run the risk of what might be related" because "I could not give up all my own notions of what I think everybody owes to themselves".[49] What she owed to herself could most amply be repaid in the novels; the truth could best be told in the fiction.

3
Radical and Conservative

For contemporary readers the truth she told was correct and impeccable and certain to bring no blush to the cheek of a young person. A reviewer of *Evelina* was sure that "the father of a family will recommend it to his daughters". Readers of *Cecilia* were reassured that "the purest lessons of morality are everywhere inculcated, and no improper scenes presented to the reader". *The British Critic* commended the "excellent moral" of *Camilla*; and although, like nearly everybody, it found *The Wanderer* "tedious and tiresome", the novel's morality was nevertheless, of "the purest nature".[1] This pure morality was to be observed chiefly in the heroines who seemed to give readers what Dr Johnson, twenty-five years before the publication of *Evelina*, had suggested that fiction should give:

> the most perfect idea of virtue; of virtue not angelical, nor above probability, for what we cannot credit we shall never imitate, but the highest and purest that humanity can reach, which, exercised in such trials as the various revolutions of things shall bring upon it, may by conquering some calamities, and enduring others, teach us what we may hope, and what we can perform.[2]

Fanny Burney was, then, for everyone a conventional, or better still, conservative novelist; the novelist may, indeed, have declined, but the moralist never moved, and as the *Quarterly Review* unkindly put it, "The Wanderer has the identical features of Evelina – but of Evelina grown old."[3] Fanny Burney's single and contemptuous reference to Mary Wollstonecraft (and Thomas Paine) seems to confirm this cautious or even reactionary· impression. She refers in 1817 (a little anachronistically: her long stay in France made her slow to appreciate current intellectual movements in England) to

> the maxims and manners of the day, which uphold not alone the Rights of Man, and the Rights of Woman, but the Rights of

Children – and will, ere long, in all probability, include the Rights of Cats, Dogs, and Mice.

(*Journals*, IX, 305)

Fanny Burney's position, however, is not likely to be so simple or so fixed, since (as we saw) her career as a novelist spanned thirty-six years from the relative social and political calm of pre-revolutionary days and the hey-day of the sentimental novel, through the turbulent, political 1790s to the defeat of Napoleon and (as she felt) of all jacobinical tendencies in England. (The Gordon Riots of 1780 had frightened her; but unlike later events in France they were only riots and not the expression of philosophies of libertinism and anarchy.)

Marilyn Butler[4] has expertly charted the opinions and attitudes of conservative and radical (or jacobin) writers (mainly novelists) from 1790 to 1816, the year in which Jane Austen wrote *Persuasion*. She has shown, too, how blurred the distinctions can sometimes be, how difficult it is in dealing with novels to outline fixed positions, or keep conservative and radical always clearly on separate sides as if they were teams in a tug of war. Nevertheless, the waters ought to be further muddied. One reason why it is hard to establish the position of various writers (principally, of course, Fanny Burney) is that we are dealing very often with novelists or with novels as evidence, and Fanny Burney herself has indirectly warned us of a problem. In 1800, in spite of incurring her father's "unaccountable but most afflicting displeasure", she wrote a comedy. She assures her father that in the play (*Love and Fashion*) he will find "nothing in the principles, the moral, or the language" to make him blush for her. But this is not the point. She does not want to upset or displease him, and she tells him that in submitting it for theatrical approval she did not run "a wanton risk" – that is, a risk which could have been avoided. But she has really no choice in what she writes for the public, and she cannot aim only to please: "My imagination is not at my own controll, or I would always have continued in the walk you approved."[5] And there is something else to confuse the way for the historian of ideas: the political patterns are less clear when the writers are women; their feminist concerns can sometimes run counter to their political and social allegiances. In the war of ideas Jane Austen will be found under the conservative banner, but it is the woman writer who allows her heroine to say in *Persuasion*:

Men have had every advantage of us in telling their own story. Education has been theirs in so much higher a degree; the pen has been in their hands. I will not allow books to prove any thing . . . All the privilege I claim for my own sex . . . is that of loving longest, when existence or when hope is gone.[6]

Two women who wrote novels, but are not novelists, seem to represent the extremes of conservative and radical, and, indeed, saw themselves in this way. The first is Hannah More, a close contemporary of Fanny Burney, a blue-stocking, evangelical friend of William Wilberforce and a mighty fighter with him for the abolition of the slave trade. To adapt E. M. Forster's phrase, she was not an enlightened woman but she sometimes held enlightened opinions. She worked tirelessly to help the poor and was generous in her giving, but believed that poverty was (for the poor) a blessing in disguise. In 1795, when the price of corn had risen sharply, she tried to show the poor "that their distresses arise nearly as much from their own bad management as from the hardship of the times".[7] The rich man in his castle should certainly feed, physically and morally, the poor man at his gate, but any suggestion that the rich should be made less rich and the poor less poor smacked of jacobinism and revolution and, worse still, Paine's *Rights of Man* against which she wrote a pamphlet (possibly at the government's request) in which she tried to introduce Burke's social and political philosophy to "the most vulgar class of readers". "Caroline," says the impeccable Sir John to his wife in Hannah More's *Coelebs*, "this is not the first time, since we have been at the Grove, that I have been struck with observing how many benefits naturally result to the poor, from the rich living on their own estates." The many benefits include a piece of ground on which to build a cottage for any servant who marries – "prudently". Hannah More wrote fifty moral or religious tracts (the two words were for her nearly synonyms), poems (many of them tracts in verse), *Sacred Dramas, chiefly intended for Young Persons* (very often tracts for the stage), books on practical piety and Christian morals, a treatise, *Strictures on the Modern System of Female Education* (1799) and (anonymously and with great reluctance) a novel, *Coelebs in Search of a Wife* (1808). With reluctance because she was afraid of failure on two fronts: "The Novel reader will reject it as dull. The religious may throw it aside as frivolous",[8] and because she feared the charge of inconsistency. She had always had a low opinion of novels and had always attacked their baleful influence. She had firmly, though generally, described in *Strictures* the damage that novels do: "the corruption occasioned by these books has spread so wide, and descended so low as to have become one of the most universal as well as most pernicious sources of corruption among us"; and she has been assured by clergymen that these "corrupt books" are even "procured and greedily read in the wards of our Hospitals".[9] The onslaught continues in *Coelebs*: novels, with few exceptions, have done "infinite mischief"; Fielding, Smollett, Sterne offer gross pictures of life; only Richardson may be safely read, since with his deeper and juster views of human nature he alone has shown "the triumph of religion and reason over the passions".[10] Not even he, however, escapes the blanket accusation that novelists have done "little justice to the clerical character" and have failed to advance "the interests of religion by personifying her amiable graces in the character of her ministers".[11] (It was another conservative novelist, Jane Austen, who declined to describe a good "English Clergyman . . . burying his own mother" and whose fictional clergymen do small justice to the clerical character. Little wonder that her references to *Coelebs* are dry: "You have by no means raised my curiosity after Caleb; – My disinclination for it before was affected, but now it is real: I do not like the Evangelicals." She knows she has misspelt the name, but Caleb has "an honest unpretending sound", whereas in Coelebs – the word means "bachelor" – there is "pedantry and affectation". A further comment, "Of course I shall be delighted, when I read it, like other people, but till I do I dislike it",[12] has, oddly, been taken as praise, as a neat admission of her own prejudice; but the tone is surely one of advance contempt for the book and for those who like it. Jane Austen knew her Hannah More and is unlikely to have had high hopes of any novel from a writer who attacked wit as the most "perilous possession" of the female mind and one which required "the severest castigation" and "the powerful curb of Christian control".[13]) For Hannah More these corrupt books (novels) teach "an unresisting submission to a feeling" and imply that feeling is irresistible and ought not to be resisted. Sterne's "corrupt" *A Sentimental Journey* was merely the worst example of "the vapid puling of the sentimental school"; but although his reign is now past, sensibility remains a dangerous foe. Novels of sensibility teach and encourage a moral lethargy, an unwise passiveness, and take no account of what she calls in *Strictures* "that natural corruption of the heart which it is one chief object of this slight work to exhibit".

The argument is a familiar one in the eighteenth-century debate between a system of ethics based on reason and one based on feeling and an innate moral sense. Shaftesbury, for example, emphasizes the importance of feeling in any system of ethics, and he was greatly scandalized (though the conservative Dr Johnson naturally was not) by Mandeville's low estimate of human nature. Jane Austen neatly summarizes the argument in *Sense and Sensibility* when Elinor suggests to Marianne that it was wrong to visit a house alone with a young man (Willoughby). Marianne answers that she never spent so pleasant a morning in her life:

"I am afraid," replies Elinor, "that the pleasantness of an employment does not always evince its propriety."
"On the contrary, nothing can be a stronger proof of it, Elinor; for if there had been any real impropriety in what I did, I should have been sensible of it at the time, for we always know when we are acting wrong, and with such a conviction I could have had no pleasure."[14]

The danger here is that reason is given no place in the making of moral choices, and there is no sense that the will may be wilful and need some sharper control than mere feeling. Ungoverned sensibility, for Hannah More, is the original cause of "some of the worst crimes, profligacy, murder and especially suicide". She does not deny the importance of feeling, but agrees with Bishop Butler and Johnson that reason and feeling are both needed in the making of all moral decisions. The sensibility must be "carefully disciplined" if a young woman is to practise self-denial and enjoy self-knowledge. Fanny Burney, who at the age of seventeen announced in her diary that she was going to "charm myself for the third time" with Sterne's *A Sentimental Journey*, could, nevertheless, say a year later that she particularly honoured those who possessed "an agonizing sensibility" but could subdue "the too exquisite refinement of their feelings".

The second woman writer is Mary Wollstonecraft (1759–97) who created scandal in her day by her liaison with Gilbert Imlay, by her *Vindication of the Rights of Woman* (1792) and by her later marriage to William Godwin (1797). Although, like Hannah More, her most important work was not fiction, she wrote two novels, *Mary* (1788) and *The Wrongs of Woman* (incomplete at her death and published posthumously in 1798). Hannah More naturally detested what this

"English Jacobin" stood for; she refused to read the *Vindication* but found plenty to scorn in *The Wrongs of Woman* and offered a summary description of the novel. As a result of Goethe's *The Sorrows of Werther* "a direct vindication of adultery was for the first time attempted by a *woman*"; and she continues:

> The female Werter, as she is styled by her biographer, asserts, in a work intitled "The Wrongs of Woman", that adultery is justifiable, and that the restrictions placed on it by the laws of England constitute one of the *Wrongs of Women*.[15]

If Hannah More had read the *Vindication* she would have found in it a powerful defence of marriage and less "medicated venom" than she expected and feared. Both women wrote; and to write anything was for women a kind of defiance. Both were deliberately writing for women; both said similar things, made similar assumptions and set out to challenge and change current ideas on the education (or lack of education) of women. The political radical and the political conservative shared a common feminism.

They both distrusted the novel and neither used the word to describe their fiction; but both saw that fiction could teach the dangers (for a young woman) of an uncontrolled sensibility and of being, in Mary Wollstonecraft's phrase "too much under the influence of an ardent imagination to adhere to common rules".[16] Godwin agreed that his wife wished to make "her story subordinate to a great moral purpose", and, indeed, in the "Preface" to the book she insists that the message is greater than the medium, for the story "ought rather to be considered, as of a woman, than of an individual". Even in the earlier novel, *Mary* (it was sub-titled *A Fiction*) novels are called the "most delightful substitutes for bodily dissipation", but in the *Vindication* the attack on fiction is ubiquitous and sharp. The "reveries of the stupid novelists" are dangerous because they corrupt taste, "draw the heart aside from its daily duties", do nothing for the understanding, and above all encourage the essential passivity of undisciplined sensibility and feelings. In *Mary* the excessive sensibility of the heroine threatens danger, but her hymn to sensibility in chapter twenty-four is not to be read ironically; Mary Wollstonecraft wrote the novel shortly after reading Rousseau's *Emile* and she greatly admired his "uncommon portion of sensibility and penetration". But between *Mary* and the *Vindication* fell Paine's *Rights of Man* (part one, 1791) and the French

Revolution; and the cult of that sensibility which in Mary's rapture is "the most exquisite feeling of which the human soul is capable", the source of the pleasure one takes in art and the natural world, is discarded. In *Mary* sensibility merely "disposes" the soul to be virtuous; it is something to be felt and "escapes discussion". Ten years on, in her later novel, Mary Wollstonecraft finds that the indulgence of a feeble and selfish sensibility is not enough: "True sensibility, the sensibility which is the auxiliary of virtue . . . is in society so occupied with the feelings of others, as scarcely to regard its own sensations."[17] Fanny Burney, too, had always distrusted sensibility for similar reasons, had always been aware of its ambivalent power (like imagination's) for good and evil. Mrs Berlinton, in *Camilla*, has most dangerously for herself a too susceptible heart which by itself can offer "no preservative against what was wrong". Camilla, too, is at the mercy of a solipsistic imagination and of "wayward Sensibility, – that delicate, but irregular power, which now impels to all that is most disinterested for others, now forgets all mankind, to watch the pulsations of its own fancies".[18] Fiction offered too many attractive examples of such yielding, pleasurable, self-indulgent sentiment ("my tears," says Henry Mackenzie's Julia de Roubigné, "fell without control, and almost without distress") and Mary Wollstonecraft was as quickly vehement in her condemnation off such sensibility as Hannah More. It was, indeed, the former who called on Dr Johnson for support. She quotes his definition of sensibility, "Quickness of sensation, quickness of perception, delicacy", and finds that it "gives no other idea than of the most exquisitely polished instinct . . . intellect dwells not there."[19] Dr Johnson had done more than define sensibility; in his antipathy to Shaftesbury and all non-rational aspects of moral theory he had given a portrait of a person of sensibility, or "feeler" (his term) in *The Idler*, No. 100:

> She daily exercises her benevolence by pitying every misfortune that happens to every family within her circle of notice; she is in hourly terrors lest one should catch cold in the rain, and another be frighted by the high wind. Her charity she shews by lamenting that so many poor wretches should languish in the streets . . .

For intelligent conservative and intelligent radical alike, the Shaftesburian cult of sentiment is close to selfishness and often signals it. (There are many examples in Jane Austen's work. Harriet

Smith's "Oh! dear yes" and "Oh! dear no" when she visits the poor, sick family with Emma show that unthinking sensibility cannot be extended to the serious distress of others; and while Mr Woodhouse is concerned that eggs should be only lightly boiled for his guests, he does what he can to delay his daughter's marriage.)

Whatever in the education of women encourages such filleted feelings is attacked by both writers; and a prime target is, naturally, poetry. In *Coelebs* Hannah More, speaking through a mentor figure, Mr Stanley, finds few things to be more deprecated for girls than "a poetical education". Poetry encourages "the uncontrolled ravings of a vagrant fancy" which destroy the will and breeds passivity, so that if a young woman falls in love she "not only submits to the destructive dominion of a despotic passion, but glories in it". In Mr Stanley's moral tale the "ardent, generous" heroine becomes "violent" and "imprudent" and the duties of the family have to be transferred to her sister. She "sets the opinion of the world at complete defiance", loses all judgment and discretion herself and despises them in others. Mr Stanley's wife, whose sensibility is properly ordered, drops "a silent tear" as she listens to the story of the "mistaken education" and "undisciplined mind" of an unhappy girl, "the energies of whose mind would," she said, "had they been rightly directed, have formed a fine character".[20] Mary Wollstonecraft's attack on poetry comes as a greater surprise. The argument is similar as she attacks men for establishing an education which makes women, as poetry and music do, "creatures of sensation" with an "overstretched sensibility" which

> relaxes the other powers of the mind, and prevents intellect from attaining that sovereignty which it ought to attain to render a rational creature useful to others, and content with its own station; for the exercise of the understanding, as life advances, is the only method pointed out by nature to calm the passions.[21]

It is the passivity encouraged by music and poetry which Mary Wollstonecraft condemns; these pastimes breed a love of pleasure so that women are for ever "on the watch for adventures instead of being occupied by duties". The echo of Hannah More is clear and occurs many times. A life of sensation and sensibility not only leads women "shamefully to neglect the duties of life" but can cause them to "plump into actual vice".[22] Dr John Gregory's *A Father's Legacy to his Daughters* (1774) was one of the most popular books on the education of young women, but Mary Wollstonecraft quarrels with him for saying that a young girl should "give the lie to her feelings". Suppression of the feelings may be recommended by men but not by women, and Hannah More and Mary Wollstonecraft urge that the feelings and sensibility be controlled but not denied. We must, through the exercise of our understanding, learn "to calm the passions"; it is, says Mary Wollstonecraft, "by struggling with them", by teaching them "to submit to necessity", that we "attain a degree of knowledge denied to the brutes".[23] Perhaps the most popular theme for radical and conservative women novelists of the period was the education of the heroine, and in nearly every case control of the passions is the prudence which alone can guarantee self-knowledge and happiness. "Whom shall one pity so much," asks Fanny Burney in 1788, "as those who neglect to habituate those impervious assaulters of all virtue and all self-denial, *The Passions*, to the control of Patience" as well as Reason;[24] and "subduing the passions" – in Hannah More's case by "the power of religion" – is the prime principle in *Coelebs*. The emphasis in these and many other writers on self-control, on control of the feelings, came from a pessimistic view of human nature and from a conviction that neither the self nor its feelings could be trusted; from a belief, however it was phrased, in human corruptibility or even original sin. It was not a feature of the earlier sentimental novelists whose authority was Shaftesbury's *Characteristics of Men, Manners, Opinions and Times* (1711). Shaftesbury's "Good Humour" (a favourite phrase) is sure that we naturally like the highest and dislike the lowest when we see them, since we have an intuitive moral sense which will naturally (again) guide our feelings into the paths of Piety and True Religion. Only "ill-humour", either natural or forced, "can bring a man to think seriously that the world is governed by any devilish or malicious power". But by the 1790s the mood has changed. We are not surprised that the evangelical Hannah More is convinced of what she calls "the doctrine of corruption", but Mary Wollstonecraft (a Christian who later slid into deism) seems to share her traditional view of the natural corruption of the heart of man (her feminism did not extend to language) or at least of some flaw which will lead him always astray. "Few can walk alone" she writes in the *Hints* which were to have been incorporated in a sequel to the *Vindication*; "The staff of Christianity is the necessary support of human weakness."[25] Her pre-revolutionary regard for Rousseau has evaporated. He is now branded as an optimist who believed that solitude was the natural state of man in which his virtues prospered, that "all *was* right originally" and that evil was introduced into the world by man. This more realistic or sombre note comes from a disillusionment with the French Revolution which she describes in her "Letter on the Present Character of the French Nation"[26] written from Paris in February 1793, one year after the publication of the *Vindication*. From her first entry into the city the contrast of riches and poverty saddened her. The Terror, of course, was still to come, but the King had been executed one month earlier and yet she finds that "the whole mode of life" makes the people frivolous and that the French are still "the most polished, most superficial and most sensual people in the world". Although "the aristocracy of birth is levelled" there is no sign of "the fair form of liberty rising" or "Virtue expanding her wings to shelter all her children." What she finds is revolution but not reform. She thought that the revolution would change human nature and that "men would labour to become virtuous"; but now "the perspective of the golden age . . . almost eludes my sight", and her "theory of a more perfect state" almost eludes her mind. She begins to fear "that vice, or, if you will, evil, is the grand mobile of action". The dawn was a false dawn and it is no longer bliss to be alive; "names not principles are changed", and the violence of revolution "has left the dregs of the old system to corrupt the new".

In her *Vindication* Mary Wollstonecraft acknowledges the genius of Rousseau; but he is the God that failed. She is weary of his stale "transient effusions of overweening sensibility" and joins with conservative women writers in attacking his views (and the views of nearly all other male writers) on the education of women. Radical and conservative share a sombre view of what marriage means for women. At the age of sixteen Fanny Burney comments on a wedding, "O how short a time does it take to put an eternal end to a woman's liberty", and in *The Wrongs of Woman* the heroine more vividly says that "marriage had bastilled me for life". This is not an attack on marriage (for Mary Wollstonecraft "the foundation of almost every social virtue") but on its transformation into a bastille built in part on the trivial views of women's education which result from male (and female) assumptions of female inferiority. Because women are deemed inferior they are denied "a proper education", which Mary Wollstonecraft sums up as "a well-stored mind"; and because they are denied "a well-stored mind" they become inferior. They learn nothing of those enjoyments which depend only "on the solitary operations of the mind" and which "enable a woman to support a single life with dignity" and acquire any of those "rich resources"[27] which will support her in later years and provide (in Jane Austen's phrase) a "preparation for the evening of life". The fear of departing from "a supposed sexual character" had led even women of sense to rest content with mere "accomplishments", the only improvements they need acquire. The heroine of *Mary* has negative good-nature; she carefully attended to "the *shews* of things; she learnt nothing of duties", and her years of youth were spent in acquiring "a few superficial accomplishments". She married for money, and as the years passed her weak constitution "so relaxed her nerves, that she became a mere nothing".[28] Perhaps remembering her own heroine, Mary Wollstonecraft gives in her *Vindication* a picture of what happens to a woman who possesses only such accomplishments:

> I once knew a weak woman of fashion, who was more than commonly proud of her delicacy and sensibility. She thought a distinguishing taste and puny appetite the height of all human perfection, and acted accordingly. I have seen this weak sophisticated being neglect all the duties of life, yet recline with self-complacency on a sofa, and boast of her want of appetite as a proof of delicacy that extended to, or perhaps, arose from, her exquisite sensibility . . .[29]

Jane Austen has dramatized such a woman in *Mansfield Park*. Lady Bertram "spent her days in sitting nicely dressed on a sofa, doing some long piece of needle-work, of little use and no beauty, thinking more of her pug than her children, but very indulgent to the latter when it did not put herself to inconvenience". In the same novel Sir Thomas Bertram ponders his failure to educate his daughters: "To be distinguished for elegance and accomplishments – the authorized object of their youth – could have had no useful influence that way, no moral effect on the mind."[30] For Mary Wollstonecraft "without knowledge there can be no morality", no chance to create "a well-regulated mind" or see (in a phrase that could well be Hannah More's, but not Jane Austen's) "the beauty of moral loveliness".[31] And such women are everywhere in this deplorable state, though the *Vindication* is directed only at middle-class women; her scheme for a woman's education requires servants, or at least, "a servant maid to take off her hands the servile part of the household business". Meanwhile what passes for female education makes for women a gilt cage and they seek only to adore their prison.[32]

It is, however, Hannah More who gives the sharpest and most specific attack on the female accomplishments which pass for education. Fanny Burney was enthusiastic about *Strictures* and found *Coelebs* a dull novel but a good book:

> a work monotonously without interest of ANY kind, yet filled with Reflexions, Maxims, moral lessons, acute observations and admirable Strokes of Cleverness of every sort – though all so ill and unskilfully combined or intermixt, as to make a *whole* that is the quintessence of lead, while the parts frequently deserve a setting of gold.[33]

In her "Preface" to *Coelebs* Hannah More claims that females of the higher class (she means the middle-class women for whom Mary Wollstonecraft argues) "may combine more domestic knowledge with more intellectual acquirement", may at the same time be "more knowing and more useful than has always been thought necessary or compatible", and more useful *because* more knowing.[34] (The same conviction is in the *Vindication*: "Make women rational creatures . . . and they will quickly become good wives and mothers."[35]) But at present women are permitted only "a showy education" which qualifies them for "the glare of public assemblies" and increases the possibility of their being "splendidly married". This showy education consists of "accomplishments", a term now "abused, misunderstood or misapplied":

> This word in its original meaning signifies *completeness, perfection.* But I may safely appeal to the observation of mankind, whether they do not meet with swarms of youthful females, issuing from our boarding-schools, as well as emerging from the more private scenes of domestic education, who are introduced into the world under the broad and universal title of *accomplished young ladies*, of *all* of whom it cannot very truly and correctly be pronounced, that they illustrate the definition by a completeness which leaves nothing to be added, and a perfection which leaves nothing to be desired.[36]

This "phrenzy of accomplishments" was once confined to women of rank and fortune but now "rages downward with increasing and destructive violence" to the middle class; and these accomplishments which now spread like "an epidemical mania" are "the use of the pencil, the performance of exquisite but unnecessary foreign languages and of music". Mary Wollstonecraft, too, wanted to get rid of music in education as it encouraged a sensibility which "relaxes the other powers of the mind". Fanny Price was condemned by the Bertram sisters because she did not want to learn either music or drawing. Above all, accomplishments do nothing to exercise the judgment, "nor bring into action those powers which fit the heart and mind for the occupations of life"; they neither train the mind nor encourage common sense, "that experimental logic . . . compounded of observation and reflection". For both women the great aim of education is intellectual and moral – the two are scarcely separated. "The most perfect education . . . is such an exercise of the understanding as is best calculated to strengthen the body and form the heart." The words are Mary Wollstonecraft's but the sentiment is also Hannah More's. Mary Wollstonecraft insists on the need for physical exercise for girls and Hannah More does not, but it is another conservative writer who attacks schools "where young ladies for enormous pay might be screwed out of health and into vanity" and who approves of the school-mistress (Mrs Goddard) who gave the children "plenty of wholesome food" and "let them run about a great deal in the summer".[37]

Though neither Hannah More nor Mary Wollstonecraft mentions him, the common background to their proposals and strictures is Locke's immensely popular *Some Thoughts Concerning Education*, published in 1693 but influential throughout the century. Locke, of course, was concerned only with the education of boys, or "how a young gentleman should be brought up from his infancy", but it is part of the daring of the two women writers that they could see Locke's principles as equally right and fitting for young women. It is not merely that they accepted Locke's strictures on poetry and music and his doubts about the worthwhileness of learning foreign languages; like him they saw that these accomplishments were distractions from the true business of education; with him they would have agreed that the four great objects of education should be "virtue, wisdom, breeding and learning". In all three the emphasis is on the education of all the faculties and not only on the child's intellectual development. Locke puts learning last; too much emphasis was placed on this in the education of boys and he insists that it is subservient to greater qualities: "I imagine you would think him a very foolish fellow that shall not value a virtuous or wise man infinitely before a great scholar."[38] Hannah More and Mary Wollstonecraft, pleading for the better education of women who are denied all serious instruction, lay more stress on learning, but, like Locke, say little about the contents of any syllabus. "The grand end" of any education for women, says Mary Wollstonecraft, "should be to unfold their own faculties, and acquire the dignity of conscious virtue". Hannah More calls education

> not that which is made up of the shreds and patches of useless arts, but that which inculcates principles, polishes taste, regulates temper, cultivates reason, subdues the passions, directs the feelings, habituates to reflection, trains to self denial.[39]

The chief business of education is "to implant ideas, to communicate knowledge . . . to fit us for life",[40] to remind women that they are above all else rational and moral creatures and thus far no different from men. Thus far may not be far enough for Mary Wollstonecraft, but for her, too, the aims of education are the exercise of reason, the acquirement of virtue, the attaining of knowledge and, supremely, the self-knowledge that comes from struggling with and controlling our passions.[41] For Mary Wollstonecraft education should enable woman to become the companion of man; but by teaching her *why* she should be virtuous it will also show her where her duty lies – in being a good wife and mother.[42] Both women, in fact, stress the differences between the sexes, and in similar terms. Both claim "true tenderness" and "compassion" as especially female qualities (though in Hannah More's phrase, "to be silly makes no necessary part of softness") and both offer similar descriptions of sexual love in women. For Hannah More it is "not an ungovernable impulse, but a sentiment arising out of qualities calculated to inspire attachment in persons under the dominion of reason and religion". For Mary Wollstonecraft love's "tumultuous passion" must be restrained; it must acquire "serious dignity" and, through virtue, that "true delicacy" which in chapter seven of the *Vindication* she calls modesty. Modesty is neither bashfulness nor humility, but "the sacred offspring of sensibility and reason"; only a reformed education can make it flower in women, for "it is something nobler than innocence, it is the delicacy of reflection, and not the coyness of ignorance. It is the fairest fruit of knowledge" and is "the only virtuous support of chastity".[43] The present education of women, supported by such quaint bed-fellows as Rousseau and the Scots presbyterian minister Dr James Fordyce,[44] is not only an education in vanity but an incitement to vice. All male writers on women's education since Rousseau have indicated that its "whole tendency ought to be directed to one point – to render them pleasing . . . at the expense of every other virtue".[45] Marriage cannot eradicate the habits of a lifetime: "The Woman," says Mary Wollstonecraft, "who has only been taught to please . . . will try to please other men."[46] Hannah More, in the opening words of her "Introduction" to *Strictures* (and it is her severest stricture) says the same thing more sharply:

> It is a singular injustice which is often exercised towards women, first to give them a very defective education, and then to expect from them the most undeviating purity of conduct; – to train them in such a manner as shall lay them open to the most dangerous faults, and then to censure them for not proving faultless. Is it not unreasonable and unjust, to express disappointment if our daughters should, in their subsequent lives, turn out precisely that very kind of character for which it would be evident to an unprejudiced by-stander that the whole scope and tenor of their instruction had been systematically preparing them?

The education which now prevails, she goes on "consists entirely in making woman an object of attraction"; and like Mary Wollstonecraft she wants to promote the "true dignity" of women which is born of virtue based on reason. Small wonder that Hannah More was accused of spreading Jacobinical principles and even of praying for French victory in the war[47] in spite of her obvious political conservatism and her attack on all "abettors of revolutionary principles"! And small wonder, too, that Mary Wollstonecraft, with her attack on monarchs and the hereditary principle, was called one of the "impious amazons of Republican France" in spite of her contemptuous rejection of that great fore-runner of Republican France, Rousseau, with his views on the "natural" inferiority of women and the "natural" aristocracy of men!

What both writers share is a high seriousness as they insist above all on woman's dignity, modesty and chastity and the need for continuous moral effort for the attainment of virtue. So that it would be difficult to know if it were the conservative or radical who wrote:

> Virtue, as the very word imports, should have an appearance of seriousness, if not of austerity; and to endeavour to trick her out in the garb of pleasure, because the epithet has been used as another name for beauty, is to exalt her on a quicksand; a most insidious attempt to hasten her fall by apparent respect. Virtue and pleasure are not, in fact, so nearly allied in this life as some eloquent writers have laboured to prove.[48]

The difficulty of knowing shows how hard it is to divide women writers of the period along the usual political divide. Even the most intelligent attempts to find a pattern do not show how women, like men, were changed by the events of 1789 and after – how they write one way before the Revolution and the Terror and another way after them – or that their feminist concerns often cut across their more strictly political allegiances: "The colonel's Lady and Judy O'Grady are sisters under their skins." It is not possible

> . . . to draw a critical divide . . . between the advocates of a Christian conservatism on the one hand, with their pessimistic view of man's nature, and their belief in external authority; on the other hand, progressives, sentimentalists, revolutionaries, with their optimism about man, and their preference for spontaneous personal impulse against rules imposed from without.[49]

As we have seen, Mary Wollstonecraft attacks the sentimentalists' and progressives' easy optimism about man. It is true that Mr Knightley in *Emma* insists on the primacy of the external authority of duty (a principle endlessly invoked by Mary Wollstonecraft): "There is one thing . . . which a man can always do if he chooses, and that is, his duty." But the same conservative novelist allows Anne Elliott to plead the internal authority of conscience to justify her early rejection of Captain Wentworth: "I should have suffered more in continuing the engagement than I did even in giving it up, because I should have suffered in my conscience." It is not true that the progressive novelist "suggests a victim suffering at the hands of society" and the conservative novelist "a misguided individual rebelling against it", or that for the conservative writer "society itself is the real hero".[50] It is hard to see how in *Persuasion*, which celebrates (among other things) "the holiness of the heart's affections", a trivial, bankrupt society rejected by Anne could be the real hero; and in no novel of the time is the central character shown so clearly as a victim suffering at the hands of society as Juliet in *The Wanderer*. If it is objected that *Persuasion* and *The Wanderer* come at the end of their authors' careers, that merely confirms the point that the dates of novels are important.

"What I have in view," wrote Mary Wollstonecraft of her novel-fragment *The Wrongs of Woman* (1798), is "to show the wrongs of different classes of women, equally oppressive, though, from the differences of education, necessarily various"; and the heroine, Maria, refers to "her tyrant – her husband" and asks, "Was not the world a vast prison and women born slaves?"[51] The heroine of *The Wanderer*, too, is married to a tyrant. Her secret journey from France and her wanderings in England are a five-volume attempt to escape from him; and the novel is a much more extensive picture of the wrongs suffered by "different classes of women". To place a novelist or a novel in a category is to deny her growth and change and to deny imaginative complexity to a simple work. After the publication of Mary Wollstonecraft's first novel, *Mary* (1788), came the Revolution, Paine's *Right of Man* (1791–92), Godwin's *Political Justice* (1793) and his fictional version of it, *Caleb Williams* (1794). Her second novel *The Wrongs of Woman* has been called "a revision of *Mary* in the light of *Caleb Williams*".[52] Fanny Burney's novels are also a series of revisions in response to the political and intellectual turbulence of the times.

4

The Fiction

"She may write romances and speak truth." (Sir Joshua Reynolds)

I   THE EARLY NOVELS

In delineating the Heroine of this Fiction, the Author attempts to develop a character different from those generally portrayed. This woman is neither a Clarissa, a Lady G—, nor a Sophie [the ideal female pupil in Rousseau's novel-treatise *Emile*, 1762]. It would be vain to mention the various modifications of these models, as it would to remark, how widely artists wander from nature, when they copy the originals of great masters. They catch the gross parts; but the subtile spirit evaporates; and not having the just ties, affectation disgusts, when grace was expected to charm.

Those compositions only have power to delight, and carry us willing captives, where the soul of the author is exhibited, and animates the hidden springs. Lost in a pleasing enthusiasm, they live in the scenes they represent; and do not measure their steps in a beaten track, solicitous to gather expected flowers, and bind them in a wreath, according to the prescribed rules of art.

This is not a passage from the "Preface" to *Evelina* but from Mary Wollstonecraft's "Advertisement" to *Mary* (1788) though Fanny Burney in her "Preface" makes similar points. There, too, great works of fiction are invoked to guarantee the respectability of her enterprise, though she herself aims to do something different: "I yet presume not to attempt pursuing the same ground which they have tracked." Like Mary Wollstonecraft she insists that the works of great writers should not be copied: "In books, therefore, imitation cannot be shunned too sedulously"; for a copy is further from what is natural, and like Mary Wollstonecraft she wants "to draw characters from nature". In *Evelina*, too, "the soul of the author is exhibited, and animates the hidden springs", for the heroine is a dramatized version of Fanny Burney and of the hopes and fears that always attended her entrance into the world. If Fanny Burney is more successful in this than Mary Wollstonecraft it is because she had more practice – ten years of showing in diaries and letters and journal-letters of the kind that Evelina writes, the embarrassments that attend "a cultivated understanding, and a feeling heart" in "the natural progression of the life of a young woman". Mary Wollstonecraft scorns in the "Advertisement" the "prescribed rules of art", and refers to *Mary* as "an artless tale" in which "the mind of a woman who has thinking powers is displayed". Rules of art, however, are needed to tell even an artless tale; *Mary* fails as fiction because its author believed that, by definition, an artless tale required no art at all. Fanny Burney is more cautious and sophisticated. Evelina is, like Mary, a simple, innocent girl, or in Fanny Burney's words, "artless and inexperienced"; but the artlessness of the heroine is skilfully created for us through rules of art, though not prescribed rules of fiction. For the art which creates Evelina and keeps her alive for us in vivid freshness is the art perfected in dozens of letters and hundreds of pages of diary. It is the art of the journals; and *Evelina* has remained her most popular novel for two hundred years because, more than her later fiction, it calls on the strength of that art. Alone of all her works it is in first-person narrative, journal form.

Evelina was born of the diaries and journals and shows its origins in some simple and obvious ways. Very early in the novel the fop, Mr Lovel, complains of Evelina (in her hearing): "really, for a person who is nobody, to give herself such airs". Two hundred and fifty pages and some months later she remembers the word: "Since I, as Mr Lovel says, am *Nobody* . . ."[1] and we remember that her juvenile journal, written when she was Evelina's age, was addressed to herself as "Nobody": "To Nobody, then, will I write my Journal." Evelina writes a series of journal-letters and has Fanny Burney's own astonishing gifts of memory. Mrs Beaumont describes, with a detailed account of what was said, a lengthy visit to Evelina's father, Sir John Belmont. What she has to say distresses Evelina – Sir John has refused to admit that she is his daughter – and she relates it in a hasty manner; "yet," says Evelina, "I believe I can recollect every word".[2] Fanny Burney's expertise is now made a convention of the epistolary novel. Her cousin Richard enjoyed the novel but complained that every time the hero, Lord Orville, speaks to Evelina "she is *so confused,* – that she always runs out of the room". Fanny Burney made no answer but confides to her diary a warm defence of her heroine's timidity; for it is her own timidity and her own characteristic form of escape, shown in page after page of the journals, that she is describing.[3] And Evelina's great aims (as she confesses to her guardian) and the cause of her many exquisite embarrassments, were her creator's often repeated rules of conduct:

> the desire . . . to act with uprightness and propriety, that, however the weakness of my heart may distress and afflict me, it will never, I humbly trust, render me wilfully culpable. The wish of doing well governs every other, as far as concerns my conduct,
>
> *(Evelina,* III, xi, 336)

and this entails a "struggle to acquire self-approbation". Fanny Burney reports that Mrs Thrale advised her to write for the theatre because in *Evelina* "I so naturally run into conversation". Evelina herself assures Mr Villars that she will write to him every evening of what passes during the day. Half a dozen such accounts will make up one journal-letter "and that in the same manner as, if I could see, I should tell you".[4] Evelina says in answer to her confidante's complaint of long silence, "I have, however, at present, sufficient matter for a letter, in relating a conversation".[5] The same gift is everywhere in her journals, and for her correspondents was the best thing in her letters. Mr Crisp delighted in what he called her "conversation pieces", and she was aware that her own strength in letters and journals was to "recollect as much of the conversation as I can, and make the parties speak for themselves".[6]

The form of *Evelina,* a novel told almost entirely by letters from the heroine, precludes the usual novel convention of an omniscient author. Fanny Burney drew attention to the advantages of this more subjective and innocent eye (or I), this narrating of all things through the awareness or consciousness of a young girl, with the consequent increased possibilities of delight, bewilderment and comedy of a familiar world being seen in its oddness by someone unfamiliar with it. Evelina thinks back to the happy times she spent in Lord Orville's company as "a dream, or some visionary fancy". "All I can urge," writes Fanny Burney, "is, that I have only presumed to trace the accidents and adventures to which a 'young woman' is liable. I have not pretended to shew the world what it actually *is*, but what it *appears* to a girl of seventeen."[7] It is what with her sharp ear and eye and quick feelings she does in her early journals; and a few lines earlier she confesses the near identification of the heroine of the novel with the heroine of the journals when she says of her attempt to trace a young lady's entrance into the world: "Perhaps this may seem a rather bold attempt and title for a female whose knowledge of the world is very confined, and whose inclinations, as well as situation, incline her to a private and domestic life." In her diaries Fanny Burney often says how difficult it is to find time to write up her accounts of the day. It was not a problem that hindered Pamela or Clarissa or other letter-writers in epistolary novels; but once again this first novel is closer to her journals than the conventions of fiction. In the excited wish to tell Mr Villars all about her London sight-seeing and visits she rapidly admits a difficulty and a change of plan:

> I have a vast deal to say, and shall give all this morning to my pen. As to my plan of writing every evening the adventures of the day, I find it impracticable; for the diversions here are so very late, that if I begin my letters after them, I could not go to bed at all.
>
> (*Evelina*, I, xi, 28)

The sense of excitement ("nothing but hurry and perturbation") is neatly netted by the staccato, breathless syntax of her first response to London: "This moment arrived. Just going to Drury-Lane theatre. The celebrated Mr Garrick performs Ranger. I am quite in extacy. So is Miss Mirvan."[8] It is a method she had perfected in her letters, perhaps by instinct, perhaps by Mr Crisp's instruction to avoid "stiffness and study" and not to worry about "being correct when you write to me". Forty years on and she still likes a letter "written from the thoughts that occur to the Pen at the moment", and makes a distinction between "plain prose" and "measured prose".[9] The later novels, however, were not epistolary, and too often the plain prose gave way to the measured. She seems to have felt, indeed, that *Evelina* would always be her best work and that its success depended on its autobiographical closeness to her journals and the trifling adventures of her own life. ("Send me a minute Journal of every thing," Mr Crisp told her, "and never mind their being trifles, – trifles well-dressed, are excellent food.")[10]

> I often think, when I am counting my laurels, what a pity it would have been had I popped off in my last illness, without knowing what a person of consequence I was! – and I sometimes think that, were I now to have a relapse, I could never go off with such *éclat*! I am now at the summit of a high hill; my prospects on one side are bright, glowing, and invitingly beautiful; but when I turn round, I perceive, on the other side, sundry caverns, gulfs, pits, and precipices, that, to look at, make my head giddy and my heart sick. I see about me, indeed, many hills of far greater height and sublimity; but I have not the strength to attempt climbing them; if I move, it must be downwards. I have already, I fear, reached the pinnacle of my abilities, and therefore to stand still will be my best policy.
>
> (*Diary*, I, 38)

Best, perhaps, but impossible: "Creatures who are formed for motion *must* move"; there could be no repetition of *Evelina*.

Evelina stems from the early diaries and letters. The heroine sends long letters ot her elderly guardian in which she tells in detail of her busy life in London – visits to the opera and to Vauxhall and Ranelagh – of the men and women she meets, and of the little (though not little to her) embarrassments, fears and hopes she experiences every day. Above all she transcribes the talk, the trivial chit-chat, the trading of insults, the bandying of civilities, witty talk, empty talk, persiflage, the polite talk that betrays deep feelings. Evelina does all this just as Fanny Burney wrote long letters from London to Mr Crisp and filled them with the places and people she saw and the conversations she heard. A reading of *Evelina* to a few friends and members of the family shortly after publication is interrupted by "loud bursts of laughter", but not from everybody. Kitty Cooke (a friend) seemed puzzled, and Fanny Burney guessed why: "Were she to speak her thoughts, I am sure she would ask why such common things, that pass every day should be printed."[11]

And once they were printed, what was there to say about them? Modern criticism does not always know how to handle such common things because it forgets that their origin is in the letters and diaries; it looks for the sophisticated techniques of fiction to account for the novels' success and creates them when it does not find them. It searches for the coherence of a novel instead of watching for the art of a journal-writer. Fanny Burney, it is true, added to this fictionalized journal a love-affair with a wedding at the end, and a wedding to a lord at that; but contemporary readers were not concerned and were not grateful for this imposed pattern on the everyday affairs of the book. *The Critical Review* felt that this rather marred the novel by making it like too many others. It thought that Evelina should not have married a lord; indeed, "we wish to see one novel in which there is no lord".[12] Readers of the novel showed little interest in the romance interest or in Lord Orville. The talk was all of the characters and incidents. Dr Burney predictably liked Mr Villars – "that man is always right". Mrs Thrale, who had feared that it would be "a mere sentimental business", liked the book's "probability of story", humour and pathos. A more ordinary reader, her cousin Elizabeth Burney, fairly gushed over the book, but only over the characters who were "so well drawn". Two other readers, as Fanny Burney tells us, chatted about the book: *"Miss Coussmaker.* A great deal of it is conversation – such a variety of Characters 'tis amazing I declare. *Lady Hales.* And so wonderfully well sustained they are – so mark'd – indeed there is *great genius* in it."[13] Dr Johnson was "particularly pleased with the Snow-hill scenes", Mr Smith's "vulgar gentility" the "prodigiously well marked character" Sir Clement Willoughby and "that Scotch dog Macartney". More formally he admired in *Evelina* "the knowledge of life and manners, the accuracy of observation, the skill of penetration".[14]

Eighteenth-century criticism of fiction now seems amateurish, even naive. There was little critical terminology, little attempt at a critical theory of the novel as the new literary form struggled to achieve the status of art; the best that could be managed was Fielding's "comic epic poem in prose". Yet because of this, contemporary comment on *Evelina* was shrewder and quicker to note the real merits of the work than modern criticism which does not see that the "prescribed rules" of novel criticism do not apply to the art of fictionalized journal-letters. Eighteenth-century comment was often rough and ready, but even at its roughest could readily fix on the merits of the book. In 1833 the dread John Croker (famous for his sharp attack in the *Quarterly* on Keats's *Endymion*) wrote a review of Fanny Burney's *Memoirs of Dr Burney*[15] which had appeared the previous year, and in it made a brief warts-and-all assessment of *Evelina*. The faults which he noted – "the plot is puerile enough, the denouement inevitable" – relate to the imposed romance pattern, but the merits are those of the journals:

> the vivacity of many of the descriptions, the natural though rather too broad humour, the combination of the minor circumstances, the artist-like contrast of the several characters, and, above all, the accurate and distinctive knowledge of life and manners of different classes of society.

The humour, broader than in the journals, was probably the result of Smollett's influence; but all readers liked it, and the scenes in which Captain Mirvan played tricks on Mme Duval and Mr Lovel were especially popular. It is true that many readers compared Fanny Burney casually but favourably to Richardson (Dr Johnson more cautiously found that there were "passages" in the novel that "might do justice to Richardson") but the book was more frequently talked of as a play than a novel. Her father several times interrupted his reading of the novel with the cry of "Another Coup de Théâtre" and he frequently remarked "how *dramatic* a novel it was", meaning by that its sequence of vivid scenes. He felt it could be put on the stage "just as it is, without adding or taking away *one word*", and if it had not been already published he would have "advised its being part of a Drama"; he was almost sorry, indeed, that it was not a play.[16] Another reviewer noted her great skill in "comic characters and Dialogues". There is no detailed comment in all this, but the approach of ordinary readers to the book gave them a greater insight into its spirit and method than our modern critical approaches to fiction can do.

A recent critic[17] quotes from the "Preface" to *The Wanderer* (written thirty-six years after *Evelina*) some few simple remarks on what a novel should be – "a picture of supposed, but natural and probably human existence" – applies them to the earlier novel and dignifies them as Fanny Burney's "theory of fiction". He admits that nothing in her theory shows "technical concern" but, nevertheless, finds in the novel a technical expertise worthy of Henry James. "Almost from the beginning Fanny Burney employs a double narrative vision" through the letters of the heroine and her guardian. Villars's letters "are crucial both to the structural and thematic development of the novel"; they are "the link between the social universe Evelina has just entered and the world of Berry Hill, her guardian's home from which Evelina has departed from London". Later we are told that "*Evelina* is, in fact, a serio-comic novel which partakes of two narrative movements, one intellectual or thematic and the other situational or structural, but both operating at the same time", and the structural movement is "defined by a system of balance and counterbalance, point and counterpoint". Two soon becomes three: the novel was published in three volumes but, as well as that, "the narrative centre is tripartite. Three units, comparable in length, are separated by actions of less magnitude, entr'actes that provide useful moments of contrast and stasis." Arithmetic (and geometry) become more complicated when we are told that Fanny Burney regularly juxtaposes the comic and the serious in order "to develop the tensions which are the measure of her own quest for reality".

> The result, if one were to make a chart of the double movement, might look like this: the thematic strain, pervading the entire book, would be represented by a single, continuous line, its course gradually upward; the structural elements, enforcing the thematic, would appear to be a pendulant line swinging with more or less regularity from a fixed point between the serious and the comic.

Inevitably "the precisely ordered structure" of the novel is in part the result of irony: even when the moral purpose of the book is not explicit, "irony of situation supplies the missing hortatory element", and the comic scenes, alternating with more sober scenes, "serve thematically through ironic reversal". Then comes still higher praise: the novel is seen as myth – a myth probably suggested by the first three letters of the heroine's name.

> Her entrance into the world parallels the temptation of Eve;
> unlike the biblical figure, however, she will be able to bridle her
> impulses and reach for prudential morality. . . . That she is not
> ready for the lures of a false Eden is obvious.

In other words, there is no real parallel at all between Evelina and
Eve, and if Fanny Burney had given her heroine a different name
we should never have had this talk about myth. Another critic[18]
finds that small individual scenes are "symbolic"; they point to
larger meanings and thus provide a subtle unity to the novel
which it would not have if they were read realistically and at face
value. One example offered is the race between the two old
women who are compelled to run for a bet.[19] This episode is seen
as "almost symbolic of the attitude of Sir Clement, Lord Merton,
and Lovel toward Evelina: they try to use her – and do use her as
far as they can – for their own diversion". We must see the
symbolism (the argument runs) because of the "almost Swiftian"
savagery of the satire. But there is no satire. The correct Lord
Orville does not laugh with the others (he is, in any case, not
much given to laughing) but Evelina finds that "for some time,
the scene was truly ridiculous". Even when it stops being
ridiculous she contents herself with calling the competitors "poor
women" and when the race is over goes happily to the drawing-
room for tea. Evelina is not alone in her unconcern; there is no
record of any contemporary reader being shocked or making
comparisons between Fanny Burney and Swift.

Symbolism and satire, like irony, thematic structure and the
rest have to be found, or how shall we talk about the book? But it
was not for these that Sir Joshua Reynolds sat up all night to
finish it. The point is not whether these critical comments are true
or untrue but that it is not worth the trouble to find out. They
strike without force or conviction and fail to catch the spirit or
vital quality of the novel, its fresh energy and ability to delight us;
and all this because it is seen only as a novel, and its origins in
Fanny Burney's journals and its closeness to their concerns and
method are ignored. The same critic is, indeed, aware of this from
time to time; once we have understood the "thematic direction"
of *Evelina* it "does not invite particularly subtle analysis"; and he
notes very well that the novel is built, as Fanny Burney says in
her "Preface", on "little incidents" and that "the situations are
entertaining in and of themselves". (These things characterize the

diaries and journals.) He claims that the novel is about the search for prudence and quotes Dr Johnson's definition: "wisdom applied to practice". But once again we seem to be moving a little away from the book; the description is equally true of *Tom Jones* and therefore misses the unique quality of *Evelina*. Dr Johnson's verdict on Fanny Burney's success, "What she is, she is intuitively", is nearer the mark. This does not mean that the book is "ingenuously straightforward" (though the heroine may be) or that we have to do with an untaught talent. The intuition is skilled and disciplined, the results of many years of practice as she tried to entertain her correspondents with highly edited (artistic) recreations of people, incidents, sensations and talk. In the same way as the journals, *Evelina* is, as Dr Burney said, "artful and natural". Fanny Burney did not have the sophisticated skill of later (or even contemporary) novelists, and there seems no point in trying to find them in *Evelina* to whose success such skills are irrelevant. By casting the novel in the form of a series of journal-letters Fanny Burney has ensured that the technical failures or clumsiness which mar the later fiction cannot spoil this account of how the busy world seems to a young woman. We could wish in the later novels for the device of free, indirect speech by which a writer can simultaneously give us the thoughts and feelings of a character and pass authorial judgment on them. We think, as we read the later novels, of Jane Austen who created this form of flexible, authorial control which offers two points of view – the character's and the author's – on situations, on the characters themselves and their feelings and consciousness. A first-person narrative makes this as impossible as in a journal, where instead of our judgment being guided, our feelings are released by a single, sympathetic understanding of the heroine's difficulties, and paradoxically increased by the heroine's own, often critical, awareness of what she does and says. There is not even the possible presence (as in *Moll Flanders*) of an older, quasi-authorial narrator, the heroine who in old age tells the story of her younger self and thus makes possible a critical distancing of the events narrated. The effect of Fanny Burney's journals and diaries (as we saw) was of the immediate recording of events and people and sensations even though there was, in fact, always a gap (sometimes a long one) between the thing and its narration; and this is the art and method of *Evelina*.

Some recent feminist writing throws more light on *Evelina* and the

other novels, and recognizes the closeness of the fiction and the
journals, though here, too, the wish to see Evelina and Fanny
Burney as totally representative figures makes it difficult for these
critics to see the trees for the wood of theory.

> Allowing Miss Burney to articulate repressed aspects of her
> personality, [*Evelina*] reminds us of the degree to which her
> constant professions of fear and her insistent withdrawls
> represent not true timidity but a socially acceptable device of
> self-protection.[20]

Here the facts of the novel are ignored to fit a general argument
about women's social behaviour. Evelina, like Fanny Burney, is
remarkable for her extravagant shyness, her constant anxiety states
and desperate urge to escape. Fanny Burney defended Evelina
against a charge of bashfulness by reminding the reader that her
heroine had been brought up "in the strictest retirement", "knew
nothing of the world" and that this was explanation enough for her
timidity; and she recalls her own "Preface" where Evelina was
called "the offspring of Nature, and of Nature in her simplest
attire".[21] Evelina is very much a self-portrait, though with her busy
social round Fanny Burney could not plead Evelina's ignorance of
the world. Her own hectic embarrassments and intense shyness are
vivid features of her journals and were constantly noted by family
and friends. "Poor Fan's *such* a prude",[22] said her father; so great a
prude that he knows he dare not acknowledge to her that he is
reading *Evelina*, although she knows that he is, and he knows that
she knows that he is. Anxiety, shame, fear and extreme
embarrassment are on nearly every page of her journals. When she
was Evelina's age she was invited to open a ball: "But I was
frighten'd to death, and beg'd and besought him not to begin", and
she "prevail'd, after much fuss".[23] (Even Fanny Price managed
better than this when Sir Thomas Bertram asked her to lead the
dance.) As a grown woman she confessed that "the panics I have felt
upon entering to any strange company, or large party even of
intimates, has, at times, been a suffering unspeakably, almost
incredibly severe to me".[24] Far from being "socially acceptable",
such immoderate bashfulness, which often led to unintended
rudeness, was socially entirely unacceptable.

Commitment to theory rather than honest response to the book
leads another critic to say that "All the resources of Fanny Burney's

art are used to exorcise from Evelina and Lord Orville those qualities which give life to the book and to embody them in characters who are then criticized for their boldness." (This is seen as a response to the view that the novel tries to show "the physical and psychological threats to which women generally were subjected".)[25] It is hard to understand how Evelina and Lord Orville can be brought together in this way; and it is certain that the exorcising – if any – is unsuccessful, for it is supremely Evelina, however anxious to behave well, however guilty she may feel of some indelicate behaviour, however desperate to please, who *is* the life of the book. The truth of the book is that it shows how difficult it is for Evelina to be a young lady; or, as Evelina laments: "I am new to the world, and unused to acting for myself, – my intentions are never wilfully blameworthy, yet I err perpetually!"[26] That absence of cause and effect or of any clear logic of character and event which damages the later novels and which necessitates awkward coincidence or random happening to move the story forward, does not affect *Evelina*; for Fanny Burney shows in the novel as in the early journals that there cannot be any such logic or connection, since a young woman cannot initiate action, cannot be mistress of her fate, but must reveal her helplessness and simply suffer one incident after another to unfold and involve her in spite of herself.

Evelina, like the journals, shows a woman fearful of doing wrong, fearful of losing the love and respect of those on whom she depends; but the novel goes beyond the journals in commenting on, even questioning, the very conventions which the heroine, and Fanny Burney in her journals, were desperate to uphold. It was not the anonymity of the novel which made this increased freedom possible. Fanny Burney did not really wish to remain undiscovered; she knew that such anonymity could not last, and it was, in fact, short-lived. By writing novels she could at once express herself freely and protect herself from the opinion of the world. The attention of the reader was on the characters and story and never on the writer, who especially in the first-person journal form of *Evelina* was nowhere to be found. And so instead of letting her "unconquerable repugnance" at improper behaviour make her run away from Lady Duncannon and Lady Forster, and express simple shock at Miss Bowdler's singularity, she could in her fiction stay with them a little and allow her imagination to admit other possible ways in which women might confront their destiny.

Three characters in *Evelina* from whom Fanny Burney would have run away in life, but stays with in the novel, are the bold, bad, baronet, Sir Clement Willoughby, the coarse and brutal Captain Mirvan and the satiric Mrs Selwyn. Mrs Selwyn is modelled on the Miss Bowdler of the early diaries who is

> very sensible and clever, and possesses a great share of wit and poignancy [sharpness], which spares neither friend or foe. She reckons herself superior to the opinion of the world and to all common forms and customs, and therefore lives exactly as she pleases, guarding herself from all real evil, but wholly regardless and indifferent of appearances.
>
> (*ED*, I, 231)

She has, that is, some spirit of independence, and Fanny Burney (as we saw) "can by no means approve so great a contempt of public opinion". She is, it seems, a satirist. Fanny Burney wishes she would go away, and others dread "the *lash* of Miss Bowdler's tongue". The same complaint is made against Mrs Selwyn. "She is not a favourite with Mr Villars, who has often been disgusted at her unmerciful propensity to satire",[27] and Sir Clement, too, is uneasy: "She has wit, I acknowledge, and more understanding than half her sex put together; but she keeps alive a perpetual expectation of satire, that spreads uneasiness among all who are in her presence."[28] There was no doubt at all about how a young woman was expected to behave in the presence of a rake like Sir Clement. Chastity was, of course, everything, but the reputation of being chaste was almost as important and more difficult to preserve. "Remember," says Mr Villars to Evelina, "nothing is so delicate as the reputation of a woman: it is, at once, the most beautiful and most brittle of all human things";[29] and he gives some advice on how to guard it against the assaults of those like Mr Lovel, Lord Merton or Sir Clement Willoughby:

> It is not sufficient for you to be reserved; his conduct even calls for your resentment: and should he again, as will doubtless be his endeavour, contrive to solicit your favour in private, let your disdain and displeasure be so marked, as to constrain a change in his behaviour.
>
> (*Evelina*, II, vi, 161)

The nice, defensive gradations – "reserved", "resentment",

"disdain", "displeasure" – are straight from the courtesy books, and Evelina tries, not always with success, to escape through these forms of retreat. Mrs Selwyn, however, who is always "kind and attentive" to Evelina, asserts and defends herself by satiric attack. Evelina is uneasy at Mrs Selwyn's behaviour but does not condemn it, perhaps because Mrs Selwyn's aggressive use of her understanding is more effective than her own retreat or Lord Orville's often silent disapproval. Certainly no reader can fail to cheer as Mrs Selwyn rescues Evelina from Lord Merton who has seized Evelina's hand and refuses to let it go.

> "Pray, my Lord," cried I, "let go my hand! pray Mrs Selwyn, speak for me."
> "My Lord," said Mrs Selwyn, "in detaining Miss Anville any longer, you only lose time, for we are already as well convinced of your valour and your strength as if you were to hold her an age."
>
> (*Evelina*, III, vii, 313)

Captain Mirvan and Sir Clement are much less attractive and intelligent than Mrs Selwyn, but they, too, are used to suggest criticism of the social world and of other characters in the book, and also an enviable outspokenness which women, except for the "masculine" Mrs Selwyn, dared not display. Captain Mirvan is a coarse satirist who nevertheless speaks truth. We have (if we needed it) Mr Villars's word for it: "Shall I own to you, that, however I may differ from Captain Mirvan in other respects, yet my opinion of the town, its manners, inhabitants, and diversions, is much upon a level with his own."[30] And what of the bold, bad, baronet? He knows, as the innocent Evelina does not, that Mrs Selwyn is "everywhere hated" for her satiric refusal to do and think as the world does; and he, too, offers another way of looking at things, even at that picture of stilted perfection, Lord Orville, whom jealously but accurately he calls "cold, inanimate, phlegmatic".[31] Fanny Burney's first novel is already hinting, however indirectly, at something other than the courtesy book conduct expected of men and women, and at some movement, other than endless retreat, for women in the face of a threatening world.

We cannot know if it was the end of her anonymity or the wish to do something different which caused Fanny Burney to abandon the epistolary method of *Evelina* for the third-person narrative of *Cecilia* (1782). Both changes imposed a new authorial responsibility which makes her second novel in some ways a more cautious book even though it is "a more sinister fable"[32] than *Evelina*.

Cecilia, of good family, with a large private fortune and three guardians, finds that none of these can save her from a persecution (the guardians themselves harass and betray her) that continues and intensifies through the whole novel and reaches a menacing climax only three chapters from the end. Here, distraught by her failure to find the hero, who as much as any is the cause of her misery, she finds herself unable to pay a coachman who physically detains and insults her, while other men stand around unwilling or unable to help. (Fanny Burney's heroines are never born with money problems, but money problems are frequently thrust upon them in the shape of lost purses at awkward moments.) By her own wild, hysterical efforts she escapes and seeks refuge from pursuit in a shop where, because of her distracted manner and appearance, the shopkeeper assumes she has escaped from Bedlam:

> "She's somebody broke out of a private mad-house, I dare say," said a man who had followed her into the shop; "and if you were to take care of her a little while, ten to one you'll get a reward for it."
>
> (*Cecilia*, x, vii)

She is forced upstairs, locked in a room, and in the morning is "raving with such frenzy and desperation" that her gaolers are sure she is mad and throw her a bundle of straw to sleep on. The heroine of Mary Wollstonecraft's *The Wrongs of Woman* is locked in a madhouse by "her tyrant – her husband" although she is sane. Cecilia is driven insane by a passive conformity to society's ideal of female behaviour.

Cecilia, of course, has a happy ending – hero and heroine are reunited – but it was not happy enough for some readers who wanted the heroine's lost fortune to be restored to her. When Mr Crisp made this complaint to Fanny Burney in a letter, she showed some scorn in her reply:

> I must frankly confess I shall think I have rather written a farce than a serious history, if the whole is to end, like the hack Italian operas, with a jolly chorus that makes all parties good and all parties happy!
>
> (*Diary*, II, 107)

Her present ending, she insists, is "more natural, more according to real life" than the conventional endings of the usual circulating library novels where "a marriage, a reconciliation, and some sudden expedient for great riches concludes them all alike". *Cecilia* has the marriage and the reconciliation – several reconciliations – but it is not enough to say that even before the happy marriage at the end of the novel "the illustrative episodes that cluster about the main plot insist on the desperation of women's condition".[33] The happy ending of *Cecilia*, like the happy ending of *Persuasion*, increases our sense of desperation, for it is only by the greatest good luck that such happiness is achieved in these novels or could be achieved in real life. In *Evelina* Fanny Burney had "not pretended to shew the world what it actually *is*, but what it *appears* to a girl of seventeen"; now, in a third-person narrative, she can show the world as it really is.

Cecilia's position is more difficult and uncertain than Evelina's, whose departure from home is simply for the sake of a visit to friends which leads to a jaunt to London. London is, indeed, a threatening place, but the life-line to Mr Villars is never broken and she can, if she wishes, return to the sweet, if dull, security of her guardian's home. Cecilia has been an orphan since early youth. Her uncle, a Dean, with whom she has lived for the last five years, has just died when the novel opens and she is obliged to leave the Deanery. She has no protector other than the three guardians whom she has never seen and does not know. Her departure from her home is more solemn than Evelina's and much more final. Just as our first glimpse of Christian in *The Pilgrim's Progress* is of him "standing at a certain place, with his face from his own house" and about to set out on a journey "through the wilderness of this world", so, after uttering a secret prayer in the first paragraph, Cecilia "quitted the abode of her youth, and residence of her forefathers; while tears of recollecting sorrow filled her eyes, and obstructed the last view of her native town which had excited them". She is on her own. It would have been awkward to cast the novel in epistolary form since Cecilia is an isolated heroine with no likely confidante. She is older than Evelina (almost twenty-one), just as inexperienced but less naive. As with Evelina, "a stong sense of DUTY, a fervent desire to ACT RIGHT were the ruling characteristics of her mind";[34] and because she is older "her passions were under the control of her reason, and she suffered not her affections to triumph over her princples". But even behaving in the way recommended by Hannah More and Mary Wollstonecraft does nothing to secure this pilgrim on her progress through a much larger world than the social whirl of *Evelina*. For a little while it looks as though Cecilia may be able to preserve herself and control the menacing world (as Elizabeth Bennet does) by her wit; for unlike Evelina, Cecilia is (at the beginning) a clever, ironic and critical talker. One of her guardians, Mr Harrel, is anxious that Cecilia should like the bullying, vulgar, wealthy Sir Robert Floyer.

> "Surely you can find no fault with him; he is one of the most fashionable men I know."
> "My finding fault with him, then," said Cecilia, "will only further prove what I believe is already pretty evident, that I am yet a novice in the art of admiration."
>
> (*Cecilia*, I, vi)

But examples of her witty quickness are to be found only in the opening chapters; nothing can protect an unmarried woman, not even if she is young, handsome, clever and rich.

Cecilia may soon give up her criticism of the world, but Fanny Burney does not. For the first half of the book Cecilia has enjoyed through all her distresses "the consolation of self-approving reflections". This consolation comes from the unceasing, passive sacrifice of self to the demands of society and to the expectations of how a young woman should behave. No assertion of self can be imagined or tolerated. Mrs Delvile assures Cecilia: "*You* cannot be unhappy, you have purchased peace by the exercise of virtue, and the close of every day will bring to you a reward, in the sweets of a self-approving mind."[35] But such orthodoxy fails. Cecilia is perpetually unhappy; she justly laments that "no sooner is one wound closed, but another is opened", but still there is scarcely a murmur of complaint or resentment. No one is blamed for her endless persecution and the only escape is in the temporary collapse of her reason. There is no character like Mrs Delvile in *Evelina*, and it is through her that Fanny Burney makes her protest. She tells Mr Crisp that in Mrs Delvile she meant

> to draw a great, but not a perfect character; I meant, on the contrary, to blend upon paper, as I have frequently seen blended in life, noble and rare qualities with striking and incurable defects.
>
> (*Diary*, II, 100)

She meant, that is, to draw a grey character in spite of the orthodox view that such an exercise was morally dangerous. Dr Johnson would not allow the argument that grey characters were everywhere in the world: following nature is not always the right rule.

> Many writers, for the sake of following nature, so mingle good and bad qualities in their principal personages, that they are both equally conspicuous; and as we accompany them through their adventures with delight, and are led by degrees to interest ourselves in their favour, we lose the abhorrence of their faults, because they do not hinder our pleasure, or, perhaps, regard them with some kindness for being united with so much merit.[36]

No novelist agreed with Dr Johnson, but one ex-novelist did. Henry Mackenzie had finished with fiction by 1777, but in an essay in his periodical *The Lounger* in 1785 (three years after the publication of *Cecilia*) he agrees with Dr Johnson; and by using the same quotation from Buckingham's *Essay on Poetry* that Fanny Burney had used in the "Preface" to *Evelina*, he indicates that he has a particular target in his sights:

> The reproach which has sometimes been made to Novels, of exhibiting "such faultless monsters as the world ne'er saw" may be just on the score of entertainment to their readers, to whom the delineation of uniform virtue, except when it is called into striking situations, will no doubt be insipid. But in point of moral tendency, the opposite character is much more reprehensible; I mean the character of mingled virtue and vice which is to be found in some of the best of our Novels.

That Fanny Burney is the reprehensible writer whom this poacher turned gamekeeper has in mind, is also clear in his regretful, chiding conclusion:

> I have purposely pointed my observations, not to that common herd of Novels (the wretched offspring of circulating libraries) which are despised for their insignificance, or proscribed for their immorality; but to the errors, as they appear to me, of those admired ones which are frequently put into the hands of youth, for imitation as well as amusement.[37]

When Fanny Burney received a complaint of this kind about Mrs Delvile from Mr Crisp, her rejection of it was swift and sharp: "Your anger at Mrs Delville's [sic] violence and obduracy are nothing but what I meant to excite; your thinking it unnatural is all that disturbs me."[38] In the more harmless world of *Evelina* the often Jonsonian characters were either black or white. Sir Clement was a rake, Mr Lovel was a fop, and very unpleasant they were. But you knew where you were with them; the respectable world endorsed your opinion of them and there was no possibility of moral confusion. Mrs Delvile, however, is the respectable world's wife, and it is the respectable in *Cecilia* who are the greatest threat to the dignity, integrity and even sanity of the heroine.

Mrs Delvile is Fanny Burney's most effective – though indirect – comment on current acceptable attitudes and values. There are, however, three characters who criticize more directly the morals and manners of society; but in every case Fanny Burney's handling of them is cautious and uncertain. There is the misanthropist, Mr Albany, whose attacks on the vanity and selfishness he sees everywhere are unambiguous, but whose extremism makes him suspect. He can do nothing to help Cecilia in any way, and Fanny Burney describes him in a letter as "the old crazy moralist".[39] Lady Honoria Pemberton is a "rattle" uninhibited by convention and undeterred by Mrs Delvile. She seems at moments to be allowing Fanny Burney to express another view. But only at moments. Mrs Delvile's condemnation of her, that she shows "what in a woman is of all things the most odious, a daring defiance of the world and its opinions",[40] is exactly Fanny Burney's own nervous response to the daring Miss Bowdler. It was safer (and more acceptable) to leave satiric comment to a man, Mr Gosport. His satire, however, is usually of a general and superficial kind. He attacks "the TON misses" and divides them into "the SUPERCILIOUS and the VOLUBLE"; among men he attacks "the sect of JARGONISTS" and (another passing fashion) "the INSENSIBILISTS". (He even tells us that Mr Albany was confined for a time "in a private mad-house".) Follies like these were always acceptable targets. Mr Gosport is a detached observer content to be amused by affectation and silliness, but with no help to give, no radical criticism of the world to offer, and with no awareness of the special restrictions and difficulties of women's social position.

II   CAMILLA (1796)

Fourteen years separate *Camilla* from *Cecilia*. In that time Fanny
Burney had in earnest made her entrance into the world. She had
passed five years at court; she had lived through the shocks of the
French Revolution, the execution of the king and queen and the
increasing political turbulence of the 1790s; and she had married the
loyalist *émigré*, d'Arblay, at both Anglican and Roman Catholic
ceremonies in the summer of 1793. The new novel is defensive,
cautious and conservative. Marilyn Butler finds in it the "thorough-
going conservative theme" of a heroine who learns to submit her
own judgment "to the supreme authority of her parents and future
husband".[41] ForPatricia Meyer Spacks the novel goes even further:
a woman must above all be humble; she must be "fearful, sweet,
ignorant and utterly dependent" and must "acknowledge the
superior wisdom of the male to whose guidance she eagerly
submits".[42] (Spacks notes with puzzled relief that this was not a
picture of the now happily married Fanny Burney.) Joyce Hemlow
claims that "The English political reaction to the French Revolution
and all its works and ways had stiffened the moral postures",[43] and
she finds this stiffening everywhere in the novel. She also suggests
that after Fanny Burney's defiance in marrying a French
constitutionalist, a very clearly moral book might bring back the
approval she had forfeited, show that in spite of marrying a
Frenchman her principles were uncorrupted and that (no doubt
against the odds) "morality might flourish in a French home".

The defensive caution and conservatism show themselves in
many ways. She does not wish the book to be called a novel; it is to
be "*sketches of Characters and morals, put in action*, not a Romance".[44] It
will be a story carefully contrived ("all wove into one") to inculcate
moral lessons and she was prepared to pay the cost of this in the loss
of "the natural ease and unaffected grace which were her greatest
charm".[45] *Camilla* alone of her works is prefaced with a paragraph
which offers sombre comment on man's perverseness of spirit and
the need to be born again. This was removed from the second
edition (1802), but the same note is heard in the opening moralizing
sentence of the novel; it is "in suffering and in feeling, in erring and
repenting, that experience comes home with conviction". Then,
too, Camilla is totally without wit. Evelina, it is true, was not a witty
heroine either, but she had sprightliness and freshness of response.
Wit, however, was a form of independent thinking, a dangerous

and subversive gift; for women (though not for men) it was what Hannah More would shortly call "a peculiarly perilous possession" demanding the "powerful curb of Christian control".[46] Other possessions are perilous too. All knowledge of the world is bad: it violates a young woman's chastity of mind. Beauty, riches, rank will make the settled security of domestic life more difficult. All these things are dangerous because they give a woman power, and a woman with power will inevitably be corrupt and (even worse) corrupting. Mrs Berlinton is "lovely in person" and "pleasing in manners", but "there is much to fear from her early possession of power". When Fanny Burney learnt of Mme de Staël's improprieties, she fled. In *Camilla* the hero's advice is the same:

> "drop, or at least suspend an intercourse too hazardous to be indulged with propriety! See what she may be sometime hence, ere you contract further intimacy. At present, unexperienced and unsuspicious her dangers may be yours. You are too young for such a risk. Fly, fly from it, my dear Miss Camilla! . . . as if the voice of your mother were calling out to caution you!"
>
> (*Camilla*, Bk VI, ch. xi)

Evelina had to learn prudence. Mr Villars warns her that when she stays with Mme Duval she will need all the prudence she can call to her aid; but, he adds, "you must learn not only to *judge* but to *act* for yourself". In *Camilla* such bold trust can no longer be allowed. Only in flight is there safety – flight which is almost a regression to the innocence of childhood, when the heroine, like Keats's Madeleine, "As though a rose should shut and be a bud again", will enjoy "the modesty of retired elegance, and the security of established respectability".[47]

The novel's conservatism shows, too, in the endless insistent moralizing. Nothing can be said, nothing can be done, nothing can happen without heavy-footed moral comment from the hero Edgar Mandlebert, the misogynist mentor Dr Marchmont or the heroine's clergyman father Mr Tyrold. Mr Tyrold, indeed, is there as a moral touchstone, as Fanny Burney's official spokesman. Camilla writes down her father's moral lessons and her sister quotes them. The moral set-piece of the book, Mr Tyrold's sermon composed especially for Camilla,[48] was so popular that it was printed separately in an anthology of writings for the guidance of young women. The sermon insists above all not on prudence, but on delicacy, draws "those boundaries which custom forbids your sex to pass" and reminds Camilla that marriage is for women an entirely "appendant state". All this is a far cry from the tough sexual equality in Mr Villars's advice to Evelina:

> Though gentleness and modesty are the peculiar attributes of your sex, yet fortitude and firmness, when occasion demands them, are virtues as noble and as becoming in women as in men: the right line of conduct is the same for both sexes . . .
>
> > (*Evelina*, II, xviii)

But as the moral conservatism or defeatism of *Camilla* became more insistent, possible other ways (than in endless retreat) by which a woman might assert herself were more powerfully suggested. The voice of female protest became more clearly heard telling a truth which could not be told in the journals, and it was the voice of Mrs Arlbery.

Mrs Arlbery is iconoclastic and satiric; "wit she possessed at will" and intelligence, good-humour and kindness. Jane Austen uses irony as a form of release and freedom: Fanny Burney uses Mrs Arlbery. Jane Austen declared that "pictures of perfection make me sick", and Mrs Arlbery makes a similar judgment on that picture of perfection, Edgar: "He has just that air and reputation of faultlessness that gives me the spleen."[49] When we first meet her she is

> not young, but still handsome, with an air of fashion easy almost to insolence, with a complete but becoming undress, with a work-bag hanging on her arm, whence she was carelessly knotting, [she] entered the ball-room alone, and, walking straight through it to the large folding glass doors of the tea-room, there stopt, and took a general survey of the company, with a look that announced a decided superiority to all she saw, and a perfect indifference to what opinion she incurred in return.
>
> > (*Camilla*, Bk II, ch. ii)

The description is a careful one. The word "insolence" is used, yet she is not, in fact, insolent; the casualness of the undress is "complete" but "becoming"; she is "alone", an appendage to no man; she has neither embarrassment nor fear at entering the ball-room alone; her "general survey" shows her unafraid, critical approach to all that she sees, and she does not care what others think of her. She is very unlike Evelina or her creator, yet Fanny Burney is careful that we shall neither misjudge nor ignore her. At one point her raillery distresses Camilla:

> "Never judge the heart of a wit," answered she, laughing, "by the tongue! We have often as good hearts, ay, and as much good nature, too, as the careful prosers who utter nothing but what is right, or the heavy thinkers who have too little fancy to say anything that is wrong."
>
> (*Camilla*, Bk ix, ch. x)

There are too many "careful prosers" in the book, and Mrs Arlbery is sharp on them all; but it is her comments on the hero (whose hesitant spying on the heroine is similar to Coelebs's in Hannah More's novel) which concern us and compel our agreement. Mrs Arlbery finds Edgar "frigid", a "piece of congelation that nothing seems to thaw", "a creature whose whole composition is a pile of accumulated punctilios". She finds him a prig: "A man who piques himself upon his perfections, finds no mode so convenient and ready for displaying them, as proving all about him to be constantly in the wrong."[50] Worst of all,

> He is a watcher; and a watcher, restless and perturbed himself, infests all he pursues with uneasiness. He is without trust, and therefore without either courage or consistency. To-day he may be persuaded you will make all his happiness; tomorrow, he may fear you will give him nothing but misery. Yet it is not that he is jealous of any other; 'tis of the object of his choice he is jealous, lest she could not prove good enough to merit it.
>
> (*Camilla*, Bk vi, ch xii)

This shrewd and accurate analysis of Edgar is one of Fanny Burney's finest passages, and the crisp vigorous prose is in striking contrast with the tired, automatic Johnsonese in which conventional attitudes are expressed; but it is merely a franker rewording of Fanny Burney's own description of Edgar when we first meet him: "His disposition was serious and meditative. . . . He was observant of the errors of others, and watched till he nearly eradicated his own."[51] Mrs Arlbery's words are spoken to Camilla, and she gives the heroine two pieces of advice which the novel explicitly condemns: "show your power"; make clear "your unbiassed preference for Mandlebert". As she listens to Mrs Arlbery Camilla is, of course, angry; but only "angry with herself to find she felt no longer angry with Mrs Arlbery".

III THE WANDERER (1814)

The *Wanderer* disappointed reviewers and the public. Fanny Burney had "sketched the whole work" in her ten-year stay in France from 1802 to 1812; it was published two years after her return to England and readers hoped for information about French manners, French politics and Fanny Burney's own thoughts and feelings about Napoleon's France. The disappointment did not surprise her; the expectations of readers were, however, founded upon "Impossibilities and Improprieties". In the preface she says that it would have been ungrateful to attack a country where for ten years she had known "nothing but felicity"; but one of the editors of the *Journals* is certainly right when he claims that "prudence and fear of reprisal occasioned Fanny Burney's discreet near silence about life under Napoleon".[52] (It was not until July, 1815, that she revealed her hatred of Napoleon and the high cost she paid for remaining unmolested in France.) The novel, in fact, has nothing to do with Napoleon's France. It is her only novel whose action takes place at a clearly specified time and the only one which refers to particular historical events. The opening sentence informs us that the story begins during "the dire reign of the terrific Robespierre" and that it is the month of December. The year must therefore be 1793. The two countries (England and France) are at war (declared by France in February of that year) and a small boat of refugees is "preparing to glide silently from the coast of France". Robespierre's name occurs again and again in the novel – Fanny Burney even reminds the reader in a note that "The period is the reign of Robespierre" – but the action of the novel passes in England, and it is only in the final pages, after the fall of Robespierre in July 1794, that the heroine is able to return for a short while to France. The novel begins with the heroine's escape to England, and contemporary readers should have known that after such an escape the heroine could not return as long as Robespierre was in power and that the action of the novel must consequently take place in England. But readers expected some sort of historical and autobiographical work and they felt cheated. Wasn't it perverse of her not to set the novel at a slightly later period, since no other woman – no other person, probably – knew so much about France under Napoleon or was so well-equipped to describe it? In fact, *The Wanderer* is profoundly historical and reveals more of its author than the earlier novels or journals do. The editor of the 1815 volume of the *Journals* notices in *The Wanderer* "a new sense of history's pervasion of even the workings of the imagination and the structures of fiction", and he quotes a comment on Mme de Staël which catches the way in which this novel is historical: she "did not simply add to the discourse on literature the *theme* of history. She was the first to grasp *all* themes historically".[53] In the case of Fanny Burney's novel, not *all* themes, but simply her one great theme of the problems, perplexities and dangers faced by women who have to make their own way in an uncertain, often hostile and threatening world which will not tolerate female independence in thought, word or deed.

The small boat making its dangerous escape to England has on board the two principal characters of the novel; these are the Wanderer herself (the heroine, Juliet), whose name is not revealed until the third volume and whose identity we do not discover until the fifth, and the anti-heroine, Elinor. It is only in the final volume that we learn that Juliet is fleeing from France to escape from a forced but unconsummated marriage to one of Robespierre's agents; but it is typical of the novel that no private life is separate from a larger public life, and that consciousness is modified by outer events. Elinor's return to England is voluntary after two years in France. She commiserates in the book with Juliet on the "foggy atmosphere" of England.

> "Oh, I don't mean alone the foggy air that [Juliet] must inhale; but the foggy souls whom she must see and hear. . . . For myself I confess, from my happiness in going forth into the world at this sublime juncture, of turning men into infants, in order to teach them better how to grow up, I feel as if I had never awaked into life, till I had opened my eyes on that side of the channel."
>
> (*The Wanderer*, I, 17–18)

Elinor comes as a revolutionary and a feminist and inevitably she attacks custom and convention; only in destroying custom and ceremony are innocence and beauty born. A moment or two after the pilot of the boat has understandably "ordered every one to keep

still, at the hazard of discovery and destruction", she announces her
mission and message. From "that side of the channel" come new
ideas, a liberal, innovative spirit, a shift in consciousness which no
defences can keep out. Elinor does not defend the Terror; but "those
excesses are only the first froth of the cauldron. When once 'tis
skimmed, you will find the composition clear, sparkling,
delicious."[54] (Elinor is certainly given all the best speeches; her
opponent's defence of a Burkean gradualism falls flat.) It is not,
however, the politics of the Revolution which interest her; what she
revels in is "this glorious epoch, that lifts our minds from slavery
and nothingness, into play and vigour".[55] Because of the
Revolution she is "awaked into life", and again and again Fanny
Burney takes an imaginative delight in showing us the spiritedness
of that awakening and the energy of that life as Elinor lives out her
"code of new ideas". "The sublimity of Revolution," she claims,
"has given a greater shake to the minds of men, than to the
kingdoms of the earth";[56] and in particular it has shaken women's
view of themselves. It has saved Elinor from a loveless marriage to
Dennis Harleigh and has allowed her to express her unreturned love
for his brother Albert.

> "But for the late glorious revolutionary shake given to the
> universe, I should, at this very moment, from mere cowardly
> conformity, be the wife of Dennis! – In spite of my repentance of
> the engagement, in spite of the aversion I have taken to him, and
> in spite of the contempt I have conceived – with one single
> exception – for the whole race of mankind, I must have been that
> poor man's despicable wife! – O despicable indeed! For with what
> sentiments could I have married him? Where would have been
> my soul while I had given him my hand? Had I not seen – known –
> adored – his brother!"
>
> (*The Wanderer*, I, 349–50)

The "sublimity of Revolution" has given her sexual and intellectual
equality with men.

> "You think me, I know, tarnished by those very revolutionary
> ideas through which, in my own estimation, I am ennobled. I
> owe to them that I dare hold myself intellectually, as well as
> personally, an equal member of the community; not a poor,
> degraded, however necessary appendant to it: I owe to them my

enfranchisement from the mental slavery of subscribing to unexamined opinions, and being governed by prejudices that I despise: I owe to them the precious privilege, so shamefully new to mankind, of daring to think for myself. But for them – should I not, at this moment, be pining away my lingering existence in silent consumption?''

(The Wanderer, I, 395–96)

The ideas are Mary Wollstonecraft's, but she would have condemned the uncontrolled sensibility which expresses them. Elinor discusses "the Rights of Woman: Rights, however, which all your sex, with all its arbitrary assumption of superiority, can never disprove, for they are the Rights of human nature".[57] One of these Rights is the Right of a woman to express her love for a man, as Elinor expresses her love for Harleigh with a frankness greater than Jane Eyre's and in phrases more extravagant than Cathy's in *Wuthering Heights*:

"Say that I adore him! That since the instant I have seen him, I have detested his brother; that he alone has given me any idea of what is perfection in human nature! And that, if the whole world were annihilated, and he remained . . . I should think my existence divine!''

(The Wanderer, I, 369)

Mary Wollstonecraft and Hannah More are both recalled when Elinor complains of the contradictory attitude of men to women: "This Woman, whom they estimate thus below, they elevate above themselves. They require from her, in defiance of their examples! – in defiance of their lures! – angelical perfection.''[58] Elinor's language is always bold and uncontrolled, but she is never refuted. The daring energy of her challenge to convention and custom is never denied. She loses her lover but not the argument. More clearly and directly than Mrs Arlbery in *Camilla*, she shows how women may come out of hiding, and without the carapace of irony. "Show your power,'' Mrs Arlbery urged Camilla; "show your unbiassed preference for Mandlebert.'' Elinor's display of power and her expressions of passion for the man she loves have an energy unmatched in the novel.

Elinor, of course, is not the heroine, but to call her the anti-heroine is misleading and wrong. The term suggests that she and Juliet (the heroine) are established in opposition as some sort of thesis and antithesis in the argument of the book; and there is much to suggest that this could have been Fanny Burney's intention. Juliet can sometimes seem as correct, passive and retreating as the heroines of the earlier novels whose anxiety to do, think and say only what is proper is their sole preservative. Juliet's correctness can become quixotic and bizarre; even the hero finds that her scruples are "a little chimerical". Yet she shows a resourcefulness and independence in escaping from France, and later from her husband when he pursues her in England, which would have been impossible for Evelina, Cecilia and Camilla.

In the opening scene of *The Wanderer* Juliet and Elinor are indeed in the same boat. Both have had experience of France and the French Revolution; both are coming to England as strangers; both are alone and both meet everywhere with insult and injury. Until the closing pages Juliet, through five long volumes, is let down, even betrayed, by the very people whom she and the reader have come to like and trust. The two women face the same alien world. Elinor asks Juliet what she intends to do in England and how she intends to live:

> Juliet answered, that her choice was small, and that her means were almost null: but when she lamented the severe DIFFICULTIES of a FEMALE, who, without fortune or protection, had her way to make in the world, Elinor, with strong derision, called out, "Debility and folly! Put aside your prejudices, and forget that you are a dawdling woman, to remember that you are an active human being, and your FEMALE DIFFICULTIES will vanish into the vapour of which they are formed."
>
> (*The Wanderer*, III, 36)

But the difficulties do not so easily (even for Elinor) vanish into vapour. Juliet finds wretchedly paid employment as companion, governess and milliner, but the single woman's lot remains intolerable:

> "Alas! deprived of all but personal resource, I fixed upon a mode of life that promised me, at least, my mental freedom. I was not then aware how imaginary is the independence, that hangs for support upon the uncertain fruits of daily exertions! Independent, indeed, such situations may be deemed from the

oppressions of power, or the tyrannies of caprice and ill-humour; but the difficulty of obtaining employment, the irregularity of pay, the dread of want, – ah! what is freedom but a name, for those who have not an hour at command from the subjection of fearful penury and distress?"

(*The Wanderer*, III, 222–3)

The novel, of course, has a happy ending: Juliet marries the hero; but this is an irrelevance, part of the romance trimming, and not what we remember. When the sound of wedding bells has died away Fanny Burney sums up Juliet's story in the closing words of the novel:

Here, and thus felicitously, ended, the DIFFICULTIES of the WANDERER; – a being who had been cast upon herself; a female Robinson Crusoe, as unaided and unprotected, though in the midst of the world, as that imaginary hero in his uninhabited island; and reduced either to sink, through inaction, to nonentity, or to be rescued from famine and death by such resources as she could find, independently, in herself.

(*The Wanderer*, V, 394–5)

She is as alone, too, as Richardson's Clarissa, but unlike her is menaced by men and women in every condition of life. There is no mentor character in *The Wanderer* as there had been in Fanny Burney's other three novels. There is no one to advise her and no one to console her; but those independent resources which sustain her are as formidable and necessary as Crusoe's. Fanny Burney's vision as we see it expressed through the troubles and travails of Juliet and Elinor is close to Godwin's in *Caleb Williams*. There, too, the hero is pursued as Juliet is pursued, and like Juliet he meets with inhumanity nearly everywhere. Fanny Burney's book, like Godwin's, offers "a powerful social mechanism and a frail but genuine human will to resist it".[59] Elinor is outspoken and rash; but Juliet, too, thinks for herself, and her thought is protest and assertion without precedent in Fanny Burney's novels. After months of silent suffering Juliet rebels:

Ought I, she cried, to submit to treatment so mortifying? Are there no boundaries to the exactions of prudence upon feeling? or, rather, is there not a mental necessity, a call of character, a cry of propriety, that should supersede, occasionally, all prudential considerations, however urgent?

(*The Wanderer*, III, 313)

That prudence which was the imperative for Fanny Burney's earlier heroines is no longer enough. It is challenged by Juliet as it is challenged by Elinor, and as it was challenged by Mary Wollstonecraft's Mary: "With these notions can I conform to the maxims of worldly wisdom? can I listen to the cold dictates of worldly prudence, and bid my tumultuous passions cease to vex me."[60] Elinor, of course, speaks her protest: Juliet only thinks it; but neither her earlier heroines nor Fanny Burney in her diaries and journals had ever dared even to think it. Not until 1815, when Fanny Burney confessed the failure of prudence and passivity as guides for female conduct. On the 3rd of July, 1815 she writes to a friend who had expressed admiration for Napoleon:

O had you spent, like me, 10 years within the control of his unlimited power, and under the iron rod of its dread, how would you change your language! by a total reverse of sentiment! yet was I, because always inoffensive, never molested: as safe There, *another* would say, as in London; but *you* will not say so; the safety of deliberate prudence, or of retiring timidity, is not such as would satisfy a mind glowing for freedom like your's: it satisfies, indeed NO *mind*, it merely suffices for *bodily* security.

(*Journals*, VIII, 282)

Albert Harleigh in *The Wanderer* comments that the French Revolution "has not operated more wonderfully upon the fate and fortune, than upon the minds and characters of those individuals who have borne in it any share".[61] *The Wanderer* illustrates this. The dates of Fanny Burney's novels are important.

Notes and References

1 INTRODUCTORY

1. *Journals*, I, 235–6.
2. Ibid., I, 253.
3. Ibid., II, 2.
4. Ibid., II, 19.
5. Ibid., II, 24.
6. *Northanger Abbey*, ch. 7. *Northanger Abbey* was probably begun in 1798, two years after the publication of *Camilla*.
7. Marilyn Butler, *Jane Austen and the War of Ideas* (Oxford, 1975).
8. T. B. Macaulay, "Madame d'Arblay", in *Critical and Historical Essays* (1843).
9. David Cecil, "Fanny Burney's Novels", in *Essays on the Eighteenth Century, Presented to David Nichol Smith* (Oxford, 1945) pp. 212–24.
10. Joyce Hemlow, *The History of Fanny Burney* (Oxford, 1958) p. 22.
11. Lillian D. and Edward A. Bloom, "Fanny Burney's Novels: the Retreat from Wonder", in *Novel: a Forum on Fiction*, vol. 12, no. 3, pp. 215–35, 1978.
12. *Journals*, XI, xxvii.

2 FACT AND FICTION

1. *Northanger Abbey*, ch. 5.
2. *The Wanderer*, I, 259.
3. *Diary*, II, 108.
4. Ibid., IV, 49.
5. Op. cit., p. 31.
6. *ED*, I, 285.
7. In *Essays on the Eighteenth Century*, op. cit., pp. 168–89.
8. *Journals*, I, xxxii n.
9. Ibid., xxxii n.
10. *Diary*, IV, 76–7.
11. Ibid., V, 137–8.
12. *Journals*, I, xxiv.
13. *ED*, I, 39.
14. *Diary*, IV, 49.
15. Ibid., IV, 76.
16. Ibid., IV, 52.

17. Ibid., iv, 54.
18. Op. cit., p. 177.
19. *ED*, ii, 94–113.
20. Ibid., ii, 1.
21. Patricia Meyer Spacks, *Imagining a Self* (London, 1976) p. 159.
22. John Butt (edited and completed by Geoffrey Carnall) *Oxford History of English Literature*, (vol. viii) *The Mid-Eighteenth Century* (Oxford, 1979) p. 480.
23. *Diary*, i, 323–4.
24. *The Wanderer*, v, 177–203.
25. *Camilla*, Bk i, ch. 7.
26. *The Wanderer*, iii, 142.
27. *ED*, ii, 47–71.
28. Butt, op. cit., p. 480.
29. Op. cit., p. 175.
30. *ED*, i, 46.
31. Spacks, op. cit., p. 175.
32. Ibid., p. 175.
33. *ED*, i, 18–21.
34. *Diary*, i, 338–9.
35. Ibid., iv, 31.
36. Suppressed diary fragment quoted by Joyce Hemlow, op. cit., p. 197.
37. *Diary*, v, 170, 173.
38. Hemlow, op. cit., pp. 201–2.
39. *Diary*, iii, 364–6.
40. Ibid., v, 138–41.
41. Ibid., v, 135.
42. Spacks, op. cit., p. 176.
43. *Diary*, v, 170.
44. *Journals*, vi, 745.
45. *Diary*, iii, 57.
46. Ibid., iv, 169; ii, 233; iii, 201.
47. *Journals*, i, 41–4.
48. Jane Austen, *Letters*, ed. R. W. Chapman (Oxford 1952) pp. 127–8.
49. *Diary*, iii, 56.

3   RADICAL AND CONSERVATIVE

1. *The Critical Review*, vol. 46, pp. 202–4; *The Critical Review*, vol. 54, pp. 214–20; *The British Critic*, vol. 8, pp. 527–36; *The British Critic* (New Series), vol. 1, pp. 374–86.
2. *The Rambler*, no. 4.
3. *The Quarterly Review*, vol. 11, pp. 124–30.
4. Op. cit.
5. *Journals*, iv, 395.
6. *Persuasion*, ch. 23.
7. Quoted in M. G. Jones, *Hannah More* (Cambridge 1952), p. 146.

8. *Coelebs*, vi.
9. *Strictures*, ch. VII.
10. *Coelebs*, ii, 167–68.
11. Ibid., ii, 1–2.
12. R. W. Chapman (ed.), *Jane Austen's Letters* (Oxford 1952), pp. 256, 259.
13. *Strictures*, 257–8.
14. *Sense and Sensibility*, ch. 13.
15. *Strictures*, p. 32.
16. *The Wrongs of Woman*, ch. 4.
17. Ibid., ch. 13.
18. *Camilla*, iv, xi.
19. *Vindication*, ch. 4.
20. *Coelebs*, ii, 244–8.
21. *Vindication*, ch. 4.
22. Ibid., ch. 13.
23. Ibid., ch. 1.
24. *Diary*, iv, 265.
25. "Hints", no. 19 in *Posthumous Works* (London 1798), vol. iv, p. 186.
26. *Posthumous Works*, vol. iv, pp. 39–51.
27. *Vindication*, ch. 2.
28. *Mary, A Fiction*, ch. 1.
29. *Vindication*, ch. 3.
30. *Mansfield Park*, ch. 2; ch. 48.
31. *Vindication*, ch. 4.
32. Ibid., ch. 3.
33. *Journals*, x, 537 n.
34. *Coelebs*, i, x.
35. *Vindication*, ch. 12.
36. *Strictures*, p. 47.
37. *Emma*, ch. 3.
38. John Locke, *Some Thoughts Concerning Education* (5th edn 1705), ed. James L. Axtell, Sect. 70.
39. *Coelebs*, i, 14.
40. *Strictures*, p. 44.
41. *Vindication*, ch. 1.
42. Ibid., ch. 12.
43. Ibid., ch. 7.
44. James Fordyce, *The Character and Conduct of the Female Sex* (1776).
45. *Vindication*, ch. 2. (See also *Coelebs*, i, 195.)
46. Ibid., ch. 2.
47. M. G. Jones, *Hannah More*, op. cit., p. 176.
48. *Vindication*, ch. 4.
49. Butler, op. cit., pp. 164–5.
50. Ibid., pp. 164, 124.
51. *The Wrongs of Woman*, ch. 1.
52. *Mary* and *The Wrongs of Woman*, ed. Gary Kelly (Oxford 1976), p. xvi.

4 THE FICTION

1. *Evelina*, I, xii; III, iii.
2. Ibid., III, xvi.
3. *ED*, II, 216.
4. *Evelina*, I, x.
5. Ibid., II, xxix.
6. *ED*, I, 285.
7. Ibid., II, 212.
8. *Evelina*, I, x.
9. *Journals*, IX, 376, 419.
10. *ED*, I, 313.
11. *Diary*, I, 39–40.
12. *The Critical Review*, vol. 46, pp. 202–4.
13. *ED*, II, 226.
14. *Diary*, II, 45, 199.
15. *The Quarterly Review*, vol. 49, pp. 97–125.
16. *ED*, II, 243–5.
17. Edward A. Bloom in his Introduction to *Evelina*, op. cit.
18. Edwine Montague and Louis L. Martz, "Fanny Burney's *Evelina*", in *The Age of Johnson: Essays Presented to Chauncey Brewster Tinker* (New Haven and London, 1949), pp. 171–81.
19. *Evelina*, III, vii.
20. Spacks, op. cit., p. 181.
21. *ED*, II, 216.
22. Ibid., II, 222.
23. Ibid., I, 32.
24. *Journals*, I, 160.
25. Susan Staves, "*Evelina*; or Female Difficulties", *Modern Philology*, vol. 73, pp. 368–81.
26. *Evelina*, III, v.
27. Ibid., II, xxx.
28. Ibid., III, xiv.
29. Ibid., II, viii.
30. Ibid., I, xxiv.
31. Ibid., III, xvi.
32. Spacks, op. cit., p. 181.
33. Ibid., p. 61.
34. *Cecilia*, I, vii.
35. Ibid., VIII, iii.
36. *The Rambler*, no. 4.
37. *The Lounger*, no. 20 (18 June 1785).
38. *Diary*, II, 100.
39. Ibid., II, 113.
40. *Cecilia*, VI, vi.
41. Op. cit., p. 140.
42. Op. cit., p. 182.
43. Op. cit., p. 249.
44. *Journals*, III, 117.

45. *The Quarterly Review*, vol. 49, p. 111.
46. *Strictures*, op. cit., pp. 257–8.
47. *Camilla*, VI, xi.
48. Ibid., V, v.
49. Ibid., V, vi.
50. Ibid.
51. Ibid., II, i.
52. *Journals*, VIII, xii.
53. Ibid., xii.
54. *The Wanderer*, I, 18.
55. Ibid., I, 19.
56. Ibid., III, 38.
57. Ibid., I, 399.
58. Ibid., III, 42.
59. Butler, op. cit., p. 75.
60. *Mary*, ch. 18.
61. *The Wanderer*, V, 385–6.

Index